A STONE IN MY SHOE

A STONE IN MY SHOE

Teaching Literacy
in Times of Change

Lorri Neilsen

PEGUIS
PUBLISHERS

Winnipeg Manitoba Canada

Several of the pieces in this collection were first published as articles in *The Reading Teacher* (International Reading Association). They have been revised and adapted for publication here.

95 96 97 98 99 5 4 3 2 1

Canadian Cataloguing in Publication Data

Neilsen, Lorraine

   A stone in my shoe

   Includes bibliographical references.
   ISBN 1-895411-73-4

1. Reading (Elementary). I. Title.

LB1573.N45   1994   372.4   C94-920265-7

Book and cover design by Laura Ayers
Illustrations from original lino cuts by Jess Dixon

Printed and bound in Canada by Hignell Printing Limited

Peguis Publishers Limited
100–318 McDermot Avenue
Winnipeg, Manitoba
Canada R3A 0A2

Toll free 1-800-667-9673

*FOR ALL THE TEACHERS IN MY LIFE,
ESPECIALLY MY CHILDREN*

CONTENTS

BRING ON THE CHILDREN

I HAD A SASSY RED PLANBOOK, a teaching certificate, and a nameplate on my door. I had a storehouse of language arts guides, a fat file of mimeographed story starters, boxes of paint and clay, and a black light poster of the Beatles. At twenty-one, I was prepared to transform children's minds through language and art. Bring on the children.

IN MY LONG-HAIRED, WIDE-EYED YOUTH, an image of the good teacher stalked the hallways of my mind, and came to bear guilt and unease. I never seemed to do it right. The good teacher filled her planbook daily with goals and objectives and doggedly, like an ant on a mission, delivered the goods by the end of the day. The paths the children and I took, however, were seldom straightforward. The good teacher also "knew his subject" (isn't that what they whispered in the staff room?); he had a stockpile of knowledge that allowed him to pull an outline, with textbook-like headings and subheads, from his brain to the page with ease. Not me. I was concerned more about the *who* (the children) and the *how* (making it to the end of the day); the *what*, I believed, could always be found in a book somewhere.

The spectre of the good teacher, like a finger-wagging parent, reminded me of my weaknesses. As I grew away from him (for some reason I always thought of a man as the ideal in those days, in spite of the numbers of women in the profession), I've learned that this mythical school-master shadowed my colleagues as well, reinforcing our collective belief that success in our profession is measured largely by unwavering focus and encyclopedic knowledge. One of my rites of passage was to recognize that teaching, like life, isn't always focused, the path always straight. Another was to value the wisdom of practice.

Early in my teaching career, I thought a lesson should have a linear, controlled quality; the end should be known from the beginning. The lesson, like the curriculum, a career, or a life, had to have a specific, predictable direction. To vary from the path, the lesson, or the norm suggested a lack of focus or control, a fickleness, a vaguely immoral or subversive nature. Even worse, it meant I was winging it, or was lost.

This belief in continuity that drives us all is deeply rooted; it affects daily and lifelong decisions and creates pressure and disappointment inside and outside the classroom. Mary Catherine Bateson (1989: 4) describes the debilitating effect of the myth of the linear goal on people's lives, claiming that as a society we see achievement as "purposeful and monolithic, like the sculpting of a massive tree trunk...rather than something crafted from odds and ends like a patchwork quilt that can warm many bodies."

The only constant in life is change, Bateson claims, and if we choose a path, we must be prepared to find it has disappeared in the underbrush. Composing a life, she argues, is an improvisatory art. As teachers, our abandoned lessons and dust-covered (or written-after) planbooks—our moments of flouting "what the book says" and capturing serendipity—should not make us feel guilty or apologetic. Teaching is often improvisation. This does not mean that it lacks focus or direction. It simply means that as we devote our time and passion to meeting goals with our students, we must recognize that the goals are mutable. They change, students change, and so do we.

...as we devote our time and passion to meeting goals with our students, we must recognize that the goals are mutable. They change, students change, and so do we.

Good teaching is not merely the successful execution of a teacher-directed plan, but the weaving of an everchanging patchwork of knowledge and understanding we create with our students in our reading and writing experiences. The most satisfying and challenging of these have a certain balance and diversity, and by our being open to learn with our students, we are open to improvise in our teaching. We watch and we listen. We take side roads that provide a different view. We teach by refocusing and redefining commitments according to the students, the time, and the resources. And the more experience we have, the more we trust ourselves to offer that book to Margaret, suggest this strategy to Juan, or leave Jesse to work alone. Experience becomes a preparation deeper and more trustworthy than words in a planbook. Experience and awareness allow us to improvise.

> We owe it to our students to be flexible, and to gain enough wisdom through experience to make the teaching and learning nourish everyone.

Teaching is like baking bread. Over the years I've learned which ingredients will blend, and how to create surprise. I can feel within moments of kneading the dough whether the yeast is working; I know where to put the bread to rise in the summer and in the winter. For years, the false promise of a good recipe for bread, just like the ideal of a good teacher, created disappointment and guilt in my kitchen and my classroom (it also created a few good doorstops). Teaching over the years has taught me that we owe it to ourselves as professionals to assert our instinct for improvising, for wandering off the recipe or the mythical garden path. We owe it to our students to be flexible, and to gain enough wisdom through experience to make the teaching and learning nourish everyone.

AS A YOUNG TEACHER, I believed good teachers were single-minded in their plans, and that they "knew their stuff." For me, that meant book knowledge, knowledge that was transmitted and received through language, spoken or written. Books. Theories. Articles. Resource guides. Words and symbols, after all, were the tools we used to communicate with one another and with our students. Indeed, to be literate was to be able to move around in words and numbers purposefully and with ease. What else was there to know?

It was a naive assumption, but the educational community has always separated knowledge, as it can be conveyed through language, from experience. By so doing, we ignore our richest source of professional understanding. As Eisner (1988: 16) says, education has been dominated by theories about how the world is, how we think, learn, read and write. These theories, which have defined educational research and conversations for some time, are stated as propositions. And, as Eisner observes, propositional language dominates because "it is the vehicle, par excellence, of precise communication." It also "focuses upon categories and thus generalizes more than it particularizes...knowledge, we are told, consists of making warranted assertions."

But what I now know about teaching reading and writing, I know not only in my mind, but in my bones. This knowing transcends words on the page and goes deep into that twilight zone that makes all researchers wary: personal knowledge. Because this wisdom of practice is difficult to see, label, measure, count, or stamp, we call it intuition, sixth sense, or—strangely, considering its status—common sense. It is the essence of good teaching, the root source of improvisation, and traditionally the most undervalued knowledge in the educational enterprise.

The wisdom of practice goes beneath, beyond, or through language, and it is profound. This knowing is messy, seldom predictable or generalizable, rarely precise, and known and learned as much through our eyes, ears, hands, heart, and soul as it is through our minds.

The wisdom of practice goes beneath, beyond, or through language, and it is profound. This knowing is messy...rarely precise, and known and learned as much through our eyes, ears, hands, heart, and soul as it is through our minds.

Describing this way of knowing is difficult, especially when again—or still—we must use words. It's the moment we know a child is engaged with the story, when decoding slides smoothly into reading. It's recognizing the complicated storyline a child intends in her drawing. It's reading a student's face as she approaches with a book and knowing, in our heart of hearts, what she wants to say. It's knowing when to change the subject. It's understanding the life, reading the pulse and the meaning beyond the desks, people, books and paper in the room. Teachers, like fish in water, are saturated with this knowing. As Elliot Eisner, Howard Gardner, and Madeleine Grumet, among others, claim, it is these forms of knowing—the artistic, the intuitive, the social, the non-propositional—that are vastly undervalued by our profession and the public.

Ways of knowing beyond propositional language infuse our stories, our insights, and our shared histories with students and colleagues. Our personal knowing is tacit, difficult to name, even more difficult to put into words. It is also highly individual.

Propositional language, and the research it writes in education, has a linear, objective quality. It has also been largely the province of men (Belenky et al 1986), although the majority of the teaching population is female. In the last decade, we have begun to read and learn from the increasing number of narrative, descriptive, and anecdotal accounts of classroom experience, all of which bring to life the sounds, images, and personalities in classrooms; and all of which demonstrate how powerful and vivid alternative ways of knowing and telling can be.

Non-propositional forms of knowing and reporting are common to women, but not unique to them. Praising Wayne Gretzky, a journalist describes the hockey player's uncanny ability to see the larger rhythms, sequences of action, and repeating patterns of the game. "He can read a configuration of players on the ice, anticipate what is likely to develop next, and react to it instantly, without pausing to think" (Whyte 1990: 23). Gretzky's "second nature" is not superhuman; it's the meeting of individual style with experience. What looks like intuition or wizardry is a deep understanding of the forces at play. Novice teachers are often bemused by experienced teachers' skill and agility in choreographing the social, personal, and environmental forces that shape learning. At twenty-one, without experience, I invested my hopes in all I had: my new red planbook, my notes, and the myth of the good teacher.

Experience makes it all look easy. She graduates from playing the scales to playing jazz. He tosses away the recipe and creates a gourmet tour de force. The good teachers, the thousands who daily guide children towards independence through literacy, are working from deeply-ingrained and hard-won personal knowledge. Such knowing and teaching is worth celebrating. Bring on the children

A STONE IN MY SHOE

THE MAN, A LOCAL PHYSICIAN, rose from the audience of parents, and waited for his presence to be felt. "What are you doing about skills? When I went to school, more time was spent on spelling, memorizing and phonics than you are spending in your classroom."

The scene is a familiar one. The teacher has been, or could be, you or me. This time, it is Pat Jones, a woman with twenty years' classroom experience who returned to school for graduate work while teaching full time. Like Pat, we have all been the target of pointed questions about our practice, and, like Pat, we hear the room fall silent while the audience of parents, administrators, colleagues or friends wait for our concise, complete, and magically-simple answer.

"You're a professional, aren't you?" Pat asked. "And you specialize, don't you?"

"Yes, I am, " he answered, and Pat thought he stood a little straighter as he spoke.

"I am a professional too," she replied, "and I specialize in knowing how children learn to read and write. What I do in the classroom is based on what I know and what I continue to learn. I would be happy to sit down with you and explain why I make the decisions I do about your child's learning."

Pat told the graduate seminar group later that she had not only surprised the parent with her comments, but herself as well. She wasn't defensive, the man's combative tone changed and a conversation began.

Earning professional status is never as simple as announcing it, and yet Pat's direct and reasoned reply made public the private voice that had become her own. Daily I hear and see the signs of professional confidence emerging in a field where once it lay fallow. Signs, perhaps, that society's most beleaguered profession may now be coming into its own. As reading and writing teachers, we are not only accepting, we are inviting the challenge of change, and creating a collective sensibility marked by enthusiasm, critical awareness, courage, and understanding.

As reading professionals, we are in an age, as the Chinese legend has it, of the turbulent mirror—order and chaos on either side of the glass—and as we pass through the mirror we see the world differently. The passage teaches us that instability and change are constants; that learning and teaching, for example, are in perpetual flux; that small acts of bravery in the social world, just like particulates in the atmosphere, can cause turbulence that changes the order. We learn, too, that our growth as a profession, like our place in the universe, depends greatly on our understanding and acceptance of the harmony between order and chaos.

As I hold up a mirror to the profession, I see reflections of fundamental shifts in the way we are viewing students, ourselves, and the process of learning.

REMEMBER WHEN LIFE WAS SIMPLE? Few of us do, and more of us are now admitting it, to ourselves, to parents, and to students. In a discussion on evaluating student writing, a teacher commented, "I couldn't, in all conscience, grade these papers in front of me without knowing who the student was, what her circumstances were, and what she intended to write. Even then, it's difficult. Ten years ago, I could easily have put a grade on the paper. But now, I see every piece of writing as rooted in context. Grades give a false sense of simplicity to a complex process."

> ...our growth as a profession, like our place in the universe, depends greatly on our understanding and acceptance of the harmony between order and chaos.

In other conversations, teachers similarly argue that it is simplified assumptions about literacy and learning that underlie standardized tests, many assessment and remediation procedures, curriculum directives, policies for teaching for diversity, and many popular "cookbooks" for teaching.

Knowing the complexity operating in classrooms and in interactions with students, teachers are more hesitant than ever before, to escape the necessary passage of time with predictions. Time, an essential ingredient in deepening our understanding, is hard to come by in schools. But more of us now want to take the time to listen and learn from students, to watch and to wait, rather than prematurely apply others' simple solutions or packaged promises for building a better classroom or fixing a broken reader. We are becoming justifiably wary of the "right" answer, of the newest "comprehensive" theory, of the charismatic speaker, or the catalog whose price is nothing less than our professional self-determination.

Learning to think for ourselves is becoming a priority for literacy professionals. The more we learn about children and literacy, the more we embrace complexity and difference. The more we question black-and-white answers from research, colleagues, or administrators, the more we lobby for the time it takes to do our job well. Shattered educational promises over the years have convinced us that we owe it to ourselves and our students not to simplify life or learning. Rather, we must accept the complexity of our professional lives, and take action.

FRUSTRATED WITH THE PUSH FOR TESTING, Agnes McCully and Linda Bergevin surveyed teachers in their district about standardized assessment in order to present a brief to the provincial department of education. Where once we accepted or subverted the system in which we worked, educators like Agnes and Linda are now moving to effect change on their own. The starting point, we are realizing, is not out there—in the state boards, the school administration, political offices, or publishing houses—but in ourselves, what we say and do now with our students and with each other as professionals. More than ever before, I see teachers willing to be accountable for their beliefs, eager to create their own knowledge and to take responsibility for shaping the context in which they work.

The passive educator is often the one who has stopped learning to teach. This teacher either ignores or too easily adopts others' ideas of effective pedagogy, seldom questions institutional or intellectual status quo and, as a result, often blames the child, society, or "the system" for what's wrong about education. Such a teacher has thrown in the towel professionally. This teacher, I am convinced, is quietly and steadily being replaced by motivated teachers who think and act courageously according to their students' needs and their own professional imperative.

These emerging professionals—often treated initially like staff room pariahs—flip the educational hierarchy to put students at the head. They are always asking "what if?" and, with the unabashed courage of all changemasters, they act according to universal principles of justice and care, not parochial or petty restrictions.

Obviously, we have a long way to go to accept full responsibility in a participatory democracy and to enable others to do the same (especially since a true participatory educational democracy has yet to be created). But the steps we are taking are confident and sure. We are watching ourselves teach, creating a body of classroom knowledge that articulates our experience directly and immediately. We are reading and writing more, pursuing graduate degrees in greater numbers, publishing newsletters, articles, and books. We are walking across hallways and across state and provincial lines to initiate conversations, exchange ideas, and support one another in our efforts. It's quite typical in Nova Scotia, for example, to see teachers give up their weekend, at their own expense, to attend a literacy workshop (and quite typical, too, during coffee break, to hear them evaluate the workshop not by the Monday-morning goodies it offers, but by the opportunity the workshop provides for extending and deepening their knowledge through participation).

> ...teachers who are re-assessing cherished beliefs experience the uncertainty that can bring forth innovation and change.

WHEN THEORIES COLLIDE—or, in the case of literacy education, when many theories collide—our understandings move from order to chaos. To some, the resulting state of flux is a disaster; to others it is an opportunity to see in new ways. When the old categories break down, when we move through the glass in the mirror, our conventional mindsets crumble and our complacency is shaken. The mathematician Poincare claimed his discoveries came as unexpected insights following periods of frustration and confusion. In the same way, teachers who are re-assessing cherished beliefs experience the uncertainty that can bring forth innovation and change. Our awareness of all we see and do expands. As the anthropological saying goes, we see the familiar as strange.

It's during these times, when we experience the intellectual equivalent of a stone in our shoe, that we question the status quo:

✦ Education students challenge the integrity of an autocratic professor who preaches collaboration.

✦ A reading specialist, listening to a taped interview with a student, cringes as she hears herself ask the same question in different ways to get only the answer she wants.

✦ The teacher of bilingual students challenges policy makers' assumptions about the lack of literate behavior in the home.

✦ The high school teacher catches himself referring to teachers "down" in the sixth grade, as though teaching positions should be part of the caste system.

✦ The school principal realizes her staff, not an outsider, can initiate the strongest professional development program.

As active, seasoned, and thinking professionals, we need to construct a shared reality and we are sobered by the challenges of our differences. Yet individual teachers everywhere are becoming aware of the words and acts that mark an imbalance of power, a lack of trust or mutual regard, a slight—unwitting or otherwise—to class, color, gender, and ability. We are realizing, more than ever, that the spirit of education reflects the spirit of the human condition itself. The moment a student sees in the mirror the image of her own possibility—that spark in the soul that drew us into teaching in the first place—is the moment of transformation. And that renewed hope, made deeper and more poignant by the inequalities and injustice that weaken us, is where our professional paths finally meet. And stones or not, that hope inspires the journey.

IS ANYONE LISTENING?

DO YOU KNOW ANY OF THESE PEOPLE?

✦ A woman reluctant to approach a professor about his opinion on an issue because "well, I wouldn't know what to say. I'm not very articulate."

✦ Two teachers unwilling to speak to their school district head about their research findings on standardized tests because "he dominates the conversation and never listens anyway."

✦ A teacher who lets the vote in a staff meeting be carried in favor of a decision she opposes because she "doesn't want to rock the boat. Let's face it, I have to work with these people."

Add to these events the following incident. During the Mount Saint Vincent annual summer institute for teachers, our research section was, in itself, researched, if only briefly. Our visiting observers noted that, although only five group members of twenty were male, these men spoke a disproportionate amount of time. In other words, the male teachers took—and the female teachers let them take—most of the air time.

And finally, take this hypothetical quiz. If you had to choose the names of five people well-known in the field of literacy education over the last decade, people whom you would consider spokespeople for our profession, how many of those names would be women's?

Oh, no, you're thinking; this is taking a turn in *that* direction. But bear with me. This piece is not about attacking men; it's about professional voice, about speaking out, about being heard. At a time when the reading field is rocked by divisive issues, it is important women speak and be heard as much as men. Why?

✦ The male-female difference is the most fundamental human and political difference, cutting across class, race, and cultural lines. In virtually all cultures, women are less well off economically and socially than men. If we can't begin to understand this difference, we don't have much hope for bridging other human differences.

✦ More than two-thirds of the teaching profession are women. The overwhelming majority of elementary school teachers (and reading teachers) are women. A disproportionate number of men hold senior administrative positions (at least 75 percent in most districts) and in positions of curricular and professional influence where their voices have a greater opportunity to be heard by more members of the profession.

✦ We tend to avoid talking about male-female differences. The issues embarrass many (usually women) and seem trivial to others (usually men). Such discussion, we believe, takes our attention away from other, commonly shared, non-gendered issues. The reasons we try to brush the gender issue under the carpet—it's messy, personal (like discussing religion), and emotional—are the very reasons that suggest its importance, both in the classroom and in the staff room. (The notion of gender as a continuum, and the issue of sexuality in general, is even more necessary to discuss: to ignore the more than 10 percent of our teaching and learning population who are gay or lesbian is to keep our prejudices, more than these people, in the closet.)

✦ Our professional literature is infused with the rhetoric of power: domination, empowerment, oppression, democracy, and equality. Although many use the terms loosely and fashionably (those who will always rebottle their old wine), others use the language to represent what they know to be vast differences of opportunity in education. Most of these spokespeople talking about equality are men, however. Women's relative

> Our professional literature is infused with the rhetoric of power: domination, empowerment, oppression, democracy, and equality. Although many use the terms loosely and fashionably ...others use the language to represent what they know to be vast differences of opportunity in education.

silence is rarely questioned by these liberated men, nor do these men give up the floor to women.

✦ More than ever before, teachers are assailed by criticism from the public, policy-makers, and special interest groups. Our future as a profession depends upon our ability to speak out, collectively, for what we believe, and for what we know is best for students and schools. Developing a voice, whether we are male or female, is our professional responsibility. Understanding how gender and society influence voice, therefore, is also our professional responsibility.

> Our future as a profession depends upon our ability to speak out, collectively, for what we believe, and for what we know is best for students and schools.

The notion of responsibility usually refers to a feeling of duty or obligation that guides our behavior. But responsibility also refers to our ability to respond to others, our "response-ability." Carol Gilligan's series of studies on gender show a "way of listening to differences not only between but also within the thinking of women and men" (Gilligan et al 1988: 8). As Gilligan describes it, one voice speaks of responsibility as "equality, reciprocity, justice, and rights," and one speaks of "connection, not hurting, care, and response" (Ibid.: 8). Both voices are necessary for response-able behavior.

The justice and rights perspective is most commonly held by men. From this perspective, relationships are organized in terms of equality, symbolized by the balancing of scales. Moral concerns focus on problems of oppression, of inequality, and of fairness. The individual is viewed as separate, and relationships as either hierarchical or contractual, marked either by constraint or by cooperation. The mark of mature moral judgment from this perspective is detachment, or objectivity (Ibid.).

The perspective of care is most commonly shared by women. Here, relationship "connotes responsiveness or engagement, a resiliency of connection symbolized by a network or web…the moral ideal is one of attention and response" (Ibid.: xviii). This perspective values responding to others on their own terms; we try to see and hear with their eyes and ears. When we fail to do so, we are not being responsible.

Tension exists between the two perspectives because what one perspective values (the ideal of detachment), the other considers a failure to respond to individual circumstances. And, conversely, focusing on the uniqueness of individuals (the mark of full "responseability" in the care perspective) threatens the achievement of equality and fairness from the justice perspective.

Teaching and learning together as social beings, we are responsible for fostering dialogue, for sparking and promoting the conversations that shape us and move us forward.

Teaching and learning together as social beings, we are responsible for fostering dialogue, for sparking and promoting the conversations that shape us and move us forward. If one fears speaking out at a staff meeting, is this a lapse in responsibility? Does speaking out necessarily mean we have a voice?

"The themes of silence and voice that emerge so centrally in female narratives convey…the struggle to claim a voice and the knowledge of how readily this endeavor is foiled. When someone refuses to listen…[it signals] a failure to care" (Ibid.: 17). Silence, as Gilligan argues, is often a way of maintaining integrity in the face of inattention. Why risk further invalidation by speaking out and not being heard?

Jane Hansen tells a story about a student who was astounded to have an audience become silent as she read: "You know, when people listen, you know you have something to say."

Ira Shor talks about the ways in which he aims to overcome the imbalance of talk he hears in classroom discussion. He notes "men interrupt women when women are speaking, but women don't interrupt men…most have been socialized into deferring to a man when he starts talking" (Shor and Freire 1987: 164). Shor will interrupt to remind the man that he has violated "a democratic rule that both men and women have equal rights in discussion" (Ibid.). He encourages women to speak louder because women tend to speak in a tone that does not command the attention that a man's voice does. Shor also tries "to beat the men into the conversation when the woman finishes, to invite her to say more" (Ibid.). And because he believes that the performative aspects of teaching go undeveloped, Shor also encourages men and women alike to take drama and voice lessons so that they may "do daring things with words to create classroom discourse that captivates the students' attention" (Shor 1990: 349).

Shor's partner in the published discussion, Paulo Freire, responds to Shor's efforts to intervene on behalf of the women: "you must be careful not to take the responsibility on yourself for making the liberation of the women. The women must make their own liberation, with the contribution of some men who agree with them" (Shor and Freire 1987: 165).

Shor's response (and his sense of responsibility) to the differences of voice in a classroom setting falls within the gender lines Gilligan describes: he is concerned with justice, with equality of turn-taking, with fairness and democracy in classroom talk. Equality of voice then becomes equality of air time and of volume, a kind of affirmative action contract in discussion. Freire, quite understandably, is concerned that by running interference for women, Shor further weakens their position by usurping the power they should claim for themselves. To earn a voice, he is suggesting, women must detach themselves from the help of the most powerful other, in this case, the teacher.

Both Shor and Freire shape their arguments logically and fairly. Most struggles to equalize power (indeed, my very choice of the words "equalize power") come from the justice perspective. After all, the perspective underwrites employment opportunity contracts, the legal system, and no less than the constitutions of most democratic countries. It is difficult to deny the value of such attempts at achieving equality.

But we can look at issues from another perspective, one I encourage seekers of justice to explore. A Canadian Supreme Court judge, Madame Justice Wilson, recently cautioned the legal profession against relying too much on evidence instead of "getting into the skin of the litigant and making his or her experience part of your experience, and only when you have done that, to judge" (Crittenden 1990: 38).

Seeing the other perspective can be difficult to do. Gilligan describes such dual perspective-taking as similar to looking at the optical illusion of a vase which, after you blink, looks now like two faces in profile. When we see one image, we don't see the other.

Legislating equal air time will not always encourage more women to speak up. Talking over a man's voice, to claim a fair share of the discussion won't necessarily make women's opinions count. Tallying the number of times women speak doesn't address the question of whether someone out there cares to listen. And speech and drama lessons will scarcely provide women with the tacit authority they must feel to stand in front of their peers and be heard.

So what do we do? What should be done to encourage our seeing the other side of the picture, the two faces in profile? Or better, to begin to see from multiple perspectives? As Gilligan suggests, we need a new paradigm. We need to work toward recognizing our responsibility to one another as speakers and listeners, to transcend the limitations of valuing one perspective over another.

IN CONVERSATION RECENTLY, a former darling of the whole-language movement expressed his concern that current teacher education practices focus on "let's be buddies" at the expense of dealing with issues. Another male colleague critiqued research on teacher's narratives for its failure to situate the teachers' experience within a wider, political context. These observations—along with the long-standing critique of "process" and "whole language" approaches as being more warm and fuzzy than rigorous—are legitimate to these observers. They are legitimate because the observers are seeing only the vase, not two faces in profile. Enough time to view the picture, however, might allow them to see the necessity for engagement, connection, and response among people before they can take on larger, more public, challenges.

We can learn to see from both perspectives and perhaps more, if we begin to value them all. And how can we learn to do that? We can start by recognizing the following:

> We can learn to see from both perspectives and perhaps more, if we begin to value them all.

✦ The personal is political. This assertion is more than just another feminist placard to be tossed aside in favor of a more lofty pursuit, that of justice and equality. Critical reflection and action are person-specific, embedded in the context of individual lives, each of which is connected in webs to the lives of others. What is a monumental act of courage for one may be daily behavior to another. Small, private victories, like taking a stand, speaking up, learning to say no sometimes contribute more to personal growth and confidence than more public displays of voice; these victories must be acknowledged, and the importance—and the complexity—of the private arena must be accepted.

From the perspective of care, a teacher may concern herself or himself with making the professional personal; she or he wants, first of all, to get along well with people they work with daily. She may avoid competition (who has the best job, the attention of the administrator, or the best reading scores) in favor of co-operation and collaboration (how well everyone works together, whether all students enjoy reading and spend time at it, whether conversation takes place at all, whether tension exists in a group). In discussion such a teacher may concern herself less with "who is having their say" and more with whether the contribution represents an authentic attempt to bring the group together, to make all speakers feel comfortable about speaking out, to genuinely understand the perspective of the speaker and integrate it with her own.

◆ The substance is as important as the form. In her study of teachers at work, Susan Moore Johnson (1990: 218) writes of the two kinds of bonds, cultural and rational, that bring organizational order and purpose to otherwise disorderly enterprises. *Cultural bonds* "include the shared purposes, values, traditions, and history that promote harmonious behavior and a sense of community" (Ibid.). As internal links, they draw participants together "through shared meaning" and promote "commitment rather than compliance" (Ibid.). Cultural bonds are the "care and connection" perspective on organization. *Rational bonds* are regulatory: they are the rules, functions, rights, and authority that bind people by defining what they can and can't do. These bonds make sure the scales are balanced, that there is justice in the organizational structure.

Good schools require both bonds, and yet, in the typically fragmented atmosphere of the public school, an atmosphere which tends to isolate teachers from one another, cultural bonds are tenuous, if they exist at all. In the absence of a cultural bond, teachers—especially women or men whose perspective on responsibility is one of care—will often avoid speaking out in the staff room. "I just don't feel connected to the group," says one teacher. "I have to feel comfortable, as if I belong, as if we all care about what the other says, before I can speak up," says another. Such feelings of connectedness, of webs of shared meaning and experience, are too often characterized as the "touchy-feely" side of staff cohesiveness. And yet the absence of cultural bonds, and the failure to recognize their importance, may be a significant reason for the silence of many teachers.

A one-sided discussion such as the one I am having here with unknown readers necessarily simplifies a complex issue. But perhaps simply entering a discussion is a place to start. I hear the promise of a new paradigm in the words of an adolescent girl:

"That's unfair to me because you are not listening to what I am saying, and you are not treating me like someone who is allowed to have their own views and values" (Rachel, eleventh grade, as quoted in Gilligan, Lyons, and Hanmer 1990: 147).

Fairness is commonly thought of as a right, and being listened to, as a need or wish. One is justice; one is care. When the perspectives converge in the professional arena, as in Rachel's words, we hear the possibility of a fully human voice combining with others toward professional harmony.

RESEARCH COMES HOME

THE MAN I CALL UNCLE RESEARCH is a dying breed. He's the white, middle-class scholar who works in a quiet, intellectual haven, far away from the din and the dirt of the classroom environment. He acts on his theoretical hunches about how children learn to read and write, and he periodically sends his graduate students into the classroom on a data collection blitz. He sells his findings at a handsome price to those who want to produce materials based on "solid" research. We have trusted him—he *has* been our Uncle Research all these years—and we have let him take care of everything; our theories, what we consider knowledge in reading, and how inquiry is conducted.

Although Uncle Research has been doing what he considers best—and doing it well—his authority is now being questioned. His critics are calling his work paternalistic and exploitative. They claim he defends a hierarchy in education that has placed him at the top, at the well spring, and children—the recipients of the water of knowledge in educational research—at the bottom. The harshest criticism of Uncle Research comes from those who claim he doesn't ask questions that matter. If he did, he would experience for himself the sounds, the smells, and the anomalies of real classrooms. He'd get his hands dirty.

Traditionally, teachers have been inside classrooms doing the work, and outside the power structure of knowledge-making. As a result, while Uncle Research has been granted authority in education—his most visible influence has been in the development of classroom materials—teachers have largely done what they needed to anyway. Their practical knowledge and concerns have dominated their day-to-day interactions with children and print. Most teachers, hearing the phrase "recent research indicates," have responded with "that's not the way I see it" or "what difference does it make in my classroom?" Unfortunately, as Cochran-Smith and Lytle (1990: 2) state: "Those who have daily access, extensive expertise, and a clear stake in improving classroom practice have no formal way to make their knowledge of classroom teaching and learning part of the literature on teaching."

> Traditionally, teachers have been inside classrooms doing the work, and outside the power structure of knowledge-making.

Until recently, that is. Now "recent research" is as likely to be conducted and reported by teachers themselves as it is by our aging Uncle. Rejecting the way most classroom materials have characterized the reading process, and challenging the relevance of curricula in their own context, teachers are turning their doubts into action. We are now glimpsing what British educator Lawrence Stenhouse—the earliest promoter of teacher research—envisioned: a time when educational research must justify itself to teachers, not teachers to researchers. Stenhouse, who saw teachers' action research as the only means to gain autonomy in the system, aimed to make educational research more democratic.

The battle is uphill, however. As outsiders for so long, teachers have learned that those in power consciously or unconsciously rig the contest. Uncle Research claims that because teachers' knowledge is different, it is not amenable to the systematic and rigorous research methodologies required to advance the cause of education. Teacher research must fight the affirmative action battle familiar to women and minorities: to be seen as worthy they must live up to a pattern designed by white men in their own image.

> Is there a distinction... between research about education and research for education?

The debate begins: should research look for generalizable truths or will detailed accounts of classroom practice serve us better? Does "reflective practice" suggest the feminization of research, a movement away from rigor and objectivity; if so, is this dangerous? Is there a distinction, as Carr and Kemmis (1986) claim between research about education and research for education?

As Uncle Research argues these at the gates of the status quo, crowds of teachers, interested university professors, graduate students, among others, have left to build cities elsewhere. The results are nothing short of the renewal of a profession. Research has come home.

Only the teacher who has reflected on his or her practice knows the power it can have, personally and professionally. Here in Nova Scotia, reflective practice is not uncommon; indeed, the student-centered philosophy underlying much literacy education in the province makes teachers' learning a natural extension of building on the child's knowledge. Philosophically, child-centered teaching and classroom research work hand in hand. Across North America, teacher research is making a significant difference, but the significance, as many teachers will attest, isn't always measured statistically.

"WHAT I BELIEVED BECAME KNOWLEDGE." For Connie White, two years of journal-keeping, videotaping, writing, and reflecting on the reading and writing behavior of her primary (first year) students was the experience that turned her instincts and insights into knowledge, changing her assumptions and her practice forever.

But as important as the effect of classroom research on the individual teacher is its collective effect on the profession. As teachers substantiate what they know through research, they typically develop keen observational powers and a critical sensibility; they begin to trust their own knowledge and are less likely to accept, without question, the theories or claims of others. They are more likely to make independent choices in the classroom and reject curricula or materials that don't serve students well.

Teachers who reflect on their practice typically have more information to report to parents. For Connie White, "evaluation was never a problem. It just seemed like another journal page." Journals, logs or videotapes, rich with specific, detailed observations, not only engender the confidence of parents, but provide both the parents and the teacher with a fuller foundation from which to work. The parents in Connie White's community were enthusiastic and reassured about her knowledge.

> Teachers who reflect on their practice typically have more information to report to parents.

In her case, however, the decision to exchange journals with parents had an added benefit. Although she hoped to inform parents about what happens in a natural literacy learning environment, she says, "the very arrogance of it seemed to stare me in the face. I learned so much from the parents...we had indeed entered a partnership in supporting and watching their children learn." The bridge between home and school became stronger.

Teacher research not only has the potential of raising teachers' profile and esteem in the public eye, but it is becoming a common and effective means of building teacher networks and promoting professional renewal by teachers themselves.

Rhonda Baltzer, who characterizes her life before research as "kits, kits, kits!" analyzed hours of videotape turned on herself and discovered that her classroom talk was inhibiting the children's learning. The type of questions and the manner in which she asked them changed markedly afterwards, but other changes soon followed. Rhonda found herself regularly observing and recording what she was learning. She developed a series of workshops to discuss these issues with other teachers in her district.

Teacher research has the potential to bring professional development home...

Soon someone from a school district elsewhere in Nova Scotia approached her: would she provide workshop sessions for the teachers there? Rhonda's learning continues; but her research has an exponential power, providing the catalyst for others' learning. Teacher research has the potential to bring professional development home, as well.

When professionals such as these openly commit their energies to learning about their teaching, other changes follow. As an observer, guide, and sometimes, confidante, I have seen teachers grow in wisdom and confidence, learn to be eloquent speakers and group leaders, become assertive and knowledgeable advocates for change, forge new and affirming relationships, create support groups, and produce magnificent pieces of writing.

And because their professional growth has changed them at the core, the effects spill over into other areas of their lives as well. Smokers quit. The sedentary start an exercise program. I've watched professionals open up, reveal a sense of humor, dig up old dreams and revive them, and take on new challenges. Vaughn Marriott writes about his growth as a professional:

> The drudgery of complacency has been replaced with a sense of mission. During the past two years, I have experienced more professional growth than at any other period of my career. As important as this, if not more important, is the effect on me. I have juggled family, teaching, driver education, study, and a second business. All have survived and prospered. My family have understood and are proud of my efforts. My business is now formally registered. I feel more complete and confident as a person.

A fifth-grade teacher, Mary Ellen Carpenter, describes how classroom research "saved my life." She had been teaching in the same school for so many years that she was now teaching the sons and daughters of her first students. She felt stalled, professionally and personally. Learning to observe her children and respond to their needs as writers transformed her practice and renewed her enthusiasm as a teacher and a person.

Not all reflective practice is transforming, however. Often the reflection in the mirror can be profoundly disturbing. Looking at ourselves up close, we risk exposing our insecurities, revealing bad habits and dangerous biases, recognizing our own mediocrity, immaturity, or obsessive need for control. In some cases, we find the price of growth is simply too high: it means changes in cherished assumptions, breaking down old patterns and habits, recognizing the pathologies of our relationships with our colleagues, our students, and even our spouses.

Fear is not a door, but a key. Teachers who undertake their own research are not afraid to grow. Alice Walker (1988: 70) talks about growth as a process of becoming larger, spiritually, than we were before. "Whenever we grow, we tend to feel it, as a young seed must feel the weight and inertia of the earth as it seeks to break out of its shell on its way to becoming a plant. Often the feeling is anything but pleasant."

Pleasant or not, teachers are accepting the challenge to grow professionally and personally. Everyone benefits; most important, the readers and writers—the students—in classrooms across the continent who see the value the teacher places on lifelong learning. The gatekeeper to overthrow, after all, is not Uncle Research; it is the resistance to change.

GALAXIES

"WHO'S COMING TO THIS CONFERENCE ANYWAY?" The group sitting at the table looked carefully at the brochure for "Exploring our Teaching," an institute I was organizing in our province.[1]

"Teachers at all grade levels from all subject areas from places as far afield as Montreal, Albany, New York, and Cape Breton Island. All teachers who want someone to talk to about what they are doing, whether it's working with teachers at the college level or five year olds in a primary classroom. It's an opportunity for us to learn from one another." My reply sounded more like a sales pitch than an answer.

---

1. The author wishes to thank the conference participants who have given their permission to be quoted in this article.

One of the group members looked truly puzzled. She turned the pamphlet over, scrutinizing it: "Yes, I understand that, but who *important* is coming? I don't see any big names on this list." My answer may have sounded glib, but I meant it. "They're all important. It just depends on your perspective."

None of us in education can deny the inspirational value of a stimulating keynote speaker. I still remember Janet Emig's address on the tradition of writing research in Ottawa in 1979, and I mark that moment as a professional epiphany, what psychologists call a triggering event. Others, quite understandably, have been inspired by the words of Maxine Greene or Nancie Atwell. Every galaxy, including education, has its stars, the "important" people who help us mark our journeys or who cast light on our own efforts. We admire and learn from the brightest, those who work hard, meet challenges, forge new directions in our field, and shape new understandings about writing and reading. And we are wary of those who become blinded in their own light, the "rock stars" of reading who have public tantrums and demand audience quotas and exorbitant fees.

> We admire and learn from the brightest... who work hard, meet challenges, forge new directions in our field, and shape new understandings about writing and reading.

Professional opportunities available to teachers outside the school setting have traditionally been in a conference format, with a keynote, workshops, and a cast of well-known leaders in our field. These leaders have much to offer: they share valuable insights, bring teachers together in a professional forum, and draw crowds large enough to allow educational organizations or local councils to break even financially.

But teachers who are taking responsibility for their own growth are now looking to one another for opportunities to talk, exchange stories, collect data, and share resources. Now that research is coming home, teachers are beginning to look at one another as "important," to explore their own galaxies.

> ...teachers are beginning to look at one another as "important," to explore their own galaxies.

As it turned out, sixty-five important people gathered that weekend at the Oak Island Inn along the south shore of Nova Scotia. They brought questions, data, videotapes, personal journals, books, and an open mind. During Friday evening and all day Saturday the small hotel buzzed with conversation, questions, curiosity, and good will. Here, in the words of the participants, are comments on the journey exploring our teaching.

MaryAnne Carty, who stated she is just beginning to look closely at her teaching, found "the absence of lectures to be relaxing." Helen Smith found a small-group format "more conducive to reflecting on our own teaching." Agnes McCully noted: "From ingrained habit, I came expecting a keynote address, some drops of wisdom spilling from the cauldron a well-known expert has stirred. Perhaps from New Hampshire? Perhaps those listed as university professors? Consciously, I knew from reading the agenda that this would not happen, but the unconscious expectation was there. Instead, I found everyone an expert, worthy of attention, of being listened to."

Jan Michaud, like many others, had never attended a conference without "a major speaker and a very specific agenda." Lesley Smith found it "a pleasure to finally have a gathering dedicated solely to the sharing of ideas and experiences."

WHAT ARE THE IDEAS AND EXPERIENCES that shape the conversations of teachers when they get together to talk? Tony Kelly, concerned about the "warm words, gentle words, safe words" that abound in the name of learner-centered education, was heartened by a teacher's videotaped presentation of her research on her own teaching. "Work like Brenda Baltzer's showed me the tough, hard reality that truly reflective teachers are willing to penetrate, the mirrors they are willing to smash." Connie Pottie saw Rhonda's decision to examine her teaching as "a brave act," and noted "Rhonda has survived; I feel now I have a little more courage and motivation to take a step myself."

Experienced teachers like Ken Grant found the professional conversation helped him "identify and confirm the direction" of his work. Dianne Dodsworth became aware of how "increasingly resilient as a profession we are becoming; the sense of pride and professionalism is contagious." Kym Toole, commenting on the "dedicated, caring, compassionate professionals here," was moved to begin a personal journal, to "forge ahead and follow my instincts." Cindy Buterbaugh said she would return to class on Monday with a new awareness of how talk takes place in her classroom. Kathy Stocker decided to begin documenting her time with one particular student to track his social and literacy behaviors. Following Adrian Peetoom's encouragement and Connie White's example, many like Donna Myers realized that "sharing our experiences in written form may help someone else. Our stories need to be told." Dora Vaughn and others found the stories told by Linda Rief and Margaret Phinney to be "energizing."

Professionals new to teaching, such as Judy Anderson Smith (who attended with her professor, Rona Flippo), found the teacher talk to be a "gift." Debbie Breeze, who wishes such discussion took place in undergraduate programs, was "impressed with the tenacity and resourcefulness of the teachers I met here" and hopes, when she has her own classroom, to be able to emulate "their optimism, energy, and perseverance."

BUT THE CONVERSATIONS weren't all sweetness and light. Calling herself the "resident pessimist," Barb Rushton commented that teacher discussions must necessarily deal with change, "a huge area encompassing teacher change, curriculum change, parent connections, political change…and sometimes it seems too big to buck." Participants talked of overcrowded classrooms, overscheduled students, and overloaded curricula (covering the growing amount of content). Stories told of cutbacks deep to the bone, the absence of public support, the daily inequalities teachers battle in issues of gender (inside and outside the classroom), resources, and professional voice. As one teacher noted: "Because I am not treated professionally in my own school district, it is essential to know, for my own professional well-being, that there are educators somewhere who value my ideas and value me as a listener. Just as our kids need to be valued, so do we."

Jane Baskwill commented that being disheartened becomes a "way of life for some people; they feed one another and feel unable to move forward. A gathering like this can offer them another view, a helping hand or a gentle slap out of that state of immobility."

TOO OFTEN TEACHERS LOSE HEART because it is our training, traditionally, to believe we ought to have answers, not only for our students, but ourselves. But the measure of the success of a conversation can be not the number of answers we find, but the questions we generate. Judy Ballah remarked that the first session left her "frustrated that I had not learned enough. Then, as the day progressed, I realized that if I did not articulate my questions, they would not be addressed. This journey of exploration has led me to know that I ought not to go to conferences passively."

Gerry Carty observed that "a workshop with 'no experts' helps set the tone that it is okay to leave without answers." Paulette Whitman noted there was "a place for everyone, and for everyone's questions." We can "overcome, or circumvent the constraints," said Linda Bergevin, who saw "the act of gathering as signaling optimism. We haven't given up or we wouldn't be here."

Rosemary Buckley observed "there are always constraints with a system. We lay them out, see them for what they are" and do what we can. Vivian Vasquez wanted the time, after talking with others, to go back and "talk with myself." Nancy MacDonald wanted to take some of the critical issues, especially those involving high school students, and pursue them more concretely, in depth, at another gathering.

Mike Coughlan saw the conference as a rich collaboration of "human resources, possible compatriots along the road. Each of us carries our own candle and when we stand together, the way seems not quite so dark and gloomy, and we reveal a bit more of the road."

By late Saturday afternoon, as teachers loaded up their cars and lingered over conversations by the door, it was apparent to everyone that we, just like our students, don't always need a star to draw us together. As teachers, our galaxy is filled with important people, the stars young and old who are our students and colleagues. As Allan Neilsen commented: "The fact that there were no black holes of silence at any point during the conference is eloquent, compelling

> As teachers, our galaxy is filled with important people, the stars young and old who are our students and colleagues.

testimony to the appropriateness of a format that allows participants to actually confer, to identify and speculate on resolutions to frustrations, to celebrate insights and accomplishments." Ann Vibert, paraphrasing T.S. Eliot, summed up our travels well when she reminded us: "We will continue to explore and the end of our exploring will be to arrive where we started and know the place for the first time."[2]

2. After the Oak Island Inn conference I had many requests for information on how to organize such an event. Like many "grass roots" efforts, such gatherings arise from a collective need or purpose and can succeed only with local initiative. No organizational sponsorship is necessary, especially if the organization uses teachers' professional growth, not financial profit, as a yardstick of success.

OF PARACHUTES,
MOCKINGBIRDS, AND
BAT POETS

EARLY AUTUMN SCHOOL DAYS bring fresh pencils, a deeper sun, and a professional planbook open for growth. But soon the paper blizzard from outside sweeps into your classroom and steals your days of opportunity. By administrative fiat, you discover, you will be taking this workshop, the following information sessions, and that two-day in-service. Please mark the days in your calendar.

What you'd really like to do, instead, is spend the time working in your classroom, but that excuse won't fly so you convince yourself these sessions are good for you. After all, you can always learn something new. These will be days when you can sit for a change, enjoy a leisurely lunch, and even better, spend time talking with other teachers, even if it's only during coffee break. Besides, there are so many new ideas out there: how else to keep up with all the changes?

TWO IMAGES COME TO MIND when I think of what we do in the name of professional development. (I prefer the terms "renewal" or "growth"; "development" sounds somewhat like teacher-as-construction project, with blueprints and a date for a grand opening. But never mind.)

One is an image of the teacher as stoic survivor in a remote community known as the classroom, consumed with the challenges of children and learning, waiting patiently for, and gratefully accepting, the periodic arrival of intellectual supplies parachuted in from the civilized world. This image captures for me how many educational mandarins see teachers' growth and their benevolent role as shapers of the process. It is a colonial and patriarchal attitude and it is rooted in a mechanistic view of learning: theory and practice are commodities to be bought, delivered efficiently, and consumed (A. Neilsen 1988).

The other image is Randall Jarrell's Bat-poet, the little brown creature who wanted to explore its world, write poems about being a bat, and tell them to its friends. This image captures for me the spirit of self-determination that could rejuvenate our profession: we are hearing the voices of reading and writing teachers who are claiming opportunities to "read" their professional lives and "write" their own classroom experience and as a result claim the authority for their professional growth.

In countless workshops over the years, I have heard teachers voice their frustrations with accepted models for professional development. The feelings of resignation, futility, and anger that they express, however, are often masked by teachers' tendency to "be good sports" and "go with it." Demanding a say in their professional renewal, for many, would be yet another struggle for which they have neither energy nor hope for success. And yet, in a climate that calls for independent thinkers in the classroom, isn't it ironic that professional development practices don't follow suit? How often do reading and writing teachers have "topic choice" for their in-services? How many teachers have been given the paid leave and the resources to develop their own learning agenda? What does it say when our language describes teachers as being "inserviced," thus placing them both grammatically and practically in the passive voice?

> What does it say when our language describes teachers as being "inserviced," thus placing them both grammatically and practically in the passive voice?

CERTAIN THEMES CAPTURE THE ESSENCE of the parachute model of professional development. Some have become in-jokes in our field. One is the "Monday morning goodies" theme. As one teacher expressed it: "I do not want to hear about (complicated) unrealistic theories that are impossible to implement. I want the theories to be already translated into practical teaching ideas that have been proven successful with students."

Workshop leaders, and often teachers themselves who participate in such sessions, often despair at teachers' demands for "something new to try on Monday morning."

People who have the luxury of time to work through theory and its implications—usually those with no chalk dust on their clothes—can't understand why some teachers want theory already translated into practice. To the theory-holders, such teachers are participating in their own demise as thinking professionals. Cathy Hanley recalled participating in a conference at which "most of the teachers around me refused to engage with the topic. People around me were saying 'Why does he expect us to write? He's the one who's supposed to be doing the work. He's the expert.' Teachers complain about students who will not do what they want them to do and yet the majority of the teachers in this assembly were unwilling to try themselves."

And yet, from where teachers sit—too often on the receiving end—what can we expect? With too little time and too many responsibilities, it's simply easier to have someone else do the work.

The parachute delivery system is difficult to dismantle. If people have intellectual supplies parachuted in regularly, habit becomes expectation, and feelings of expectation soon turn to feelings of entitlement. How dare you cut off my supplies, just when you've made me dependent upon them? How can you ask me to translate theory to practice when you continue to bring in experts that promise to do that for me?

Which, of course, is the second cliché of professional development: The expert from fifty miles (okay, make it 200 miles) away who, because of publishing record or university research experience, is paid a handsome fee to deliver the goods with little understanding of the terrain she or he will be flown into. These leading educators are inspiring and can challenge classroom teachers in new ways; nevertheless, an unquestioned dependence on their knowledge devalues and silences the teaching wisdom and experience that sits in the audience. Further, because school districts are often swayed by bandwagons—sometimes to hefty sums in terms of their yearly budget—teachers receive mixed messages. Carol Riley, whose district promotes student-centered learning, remembers questioning the formulaic and seemingly inflexible approach to co-operative learning a visiting "expert" once promoted on behalf of the district. When Carol suggested that perhaps the model was less than "co-operative," the speaker rebuked Carol's question and called her remarks "divisive." Carol commented: "I maintain that if my remarks were divisive, then the division warrants exploration. It reminded me of a grade nine teacher who, when challenged about the correctness of something, replied that we'd learn this way now, and then later, when we knew more, we would learn the correct way." Carol's frustration is shared by thousands of teachers who know in their souls that there is no "right way" and that the discussion itself is worth more than any answer flown in from elsewhere at whatever cost.

Which brings us to the third cliché: that knowledge increases in authority as we go up that educational ladder we've constructed. We place trust, and sometimes blind acceptance, in boards of education and university researchers to set teachers' learning agenda—as though they have a direct line to Knowledge of Higher Authority—though they are removed from classroom life and can seldom predict what our needs for professional growth will be, now or next year. This paternalistic control of teachers' professional growth is poignantly expressed in a bitter joke shared by native peoples in Canada (and likely elsewhere). In essence it reads: "They taught us to bow our heads in prayer to their god, and when we looked up, our lands were gone."

While teachers' disenfranchisement is neither as glaring nor tragic as that of native peoples', it is no less real and pervasive. Knowledge from *Up There* has been the guiding force in professional development, and teachers, for lack of time, energy, voice, and opportunity, have been unable to assert that equally authoritative knowledge is *In Here*, in classroom experience and teacher wisdom. They look up, only to find their right to shape their own learning is gone.

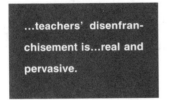
...teachers' disenfranchisement is...real and pervasive.

Again and again, I hear versions of the same:

Cathy Hanley: "For me the experiences that have made me a better teacher are the conversations with other teachers, in staff rooms, even in cars on the way to meetings"

From Janet Veitch: "Being able to discuss, question, comment, share concerns and beliefs, doubts, anxieties and successes with other teachers having a variety of backgrounds and experiences, provides a very supportive structure around which to build."

From Elsa Bond: "If we are aware (of the latest theories) we then have the power to choose what could be beneficial in our classroom. But what is more essential is getting together to talk about what works, what we are doing."

But the skies overhead still drop supplies by parachute on our schools and our minds. Professional "development" is still largely considered a packaging enterprise, more like a commodity than a way of being, a process of acquiring rather than inquiring. How do we know when we are getting what we need to grow? Discussions with teachers about the difference between what is served up on the typical in-service day and the conditions they need for professional renewal give rise to the following questions.

+ Are there people around me whose ideas cause me to reflect on my own ideas but whose conversation enables, rather than silences?

+ Is this a context where there are no right responses or perspectives (whether spoken or unspoken), only authentic ones?

+ Is what I am doing or thinking now extending my reach without causing me to lose my balance? In other words, is what I am teaching and learning challenging me, but allowing me to draw stability from my experience to date?

+ Is there a place in this community where my stories are listened to—not tolerated or trivialized or considered off topic, but listened to?

+ Is this a context in which, like an academy of the kitchen table, I can dress down, bring my sour-dough recipe, and weave theory with my daily experience?

IN RANDALL JARRELL'S GENTLE ALLEGORY (1963), the bat who decides to separate from its comfortable community stays awake in the daytime and is rewarded with sights and sounds that open up a new world for him. His friends won't join him because the sun hurts their eyes.

Hearing the song of the mockingbird, the bat decides to make up a song. But when it tries, the tune won't come. The bat decides: "If you get the words right, you don't need a tune."

The bat-poet eagerly writes poems for others: the mockingbird, the chipmunk, and the cardinal, with varying degrees of success.

When the bat captures in poetry the mockingbird's habit of driving creatures off and then imitating them, the bird's strong reaction to the bat's poem reveals its contempt for those the mockingbird imitates. The bat-poet decides to spend the rest of the season writing a poem that describes the experience of being a bat.

The richness of the allegory demands better treatment than this brief summary, but perhaps the bat-poet's experience is familiar enough to us all to imagine the possibility for our own renewal.

Karen Kerr talks about her experiences as a substitute after years of having her own classroom. She said her "tunnel vision" of one classroom gave her "no idea of what students did in classrooms before they reached me and after they left." As a substitute able to view education "more as a whole" she says her confidence grew and her perspective widened." Why, she wonders, aren't there ways that all teachers, like the bat-poet, can see the school and their teaching from a different perspective?

Our teaching, just like our conventional models for professional development, needs a good shake up now and again to awaken our senses and bring out the poetry. But viewing professional development as a delivery system for intellectually-dependent classroom technicians, importing knowledge rather than growing it locally, and failing to value classroom intuition and teacher talk—all this conventional wisdom—reveal us, in fact, as foolish and empty as the mockingbird.

> Our teaching...needs a good shake up now and again to awaken our senses and bring out the poetry.

It is the mockingbird, among all Jarrell's creatures, who should concern us. The mockingbird spends its days imitating other creatures and then driving them away. How many educational trends and "proven" methods have we, as a profession, imitated for awhile and then, in contempt for their utility, driven them away?

For if we continue to spend all our energies, like the mockingbird, learning to imitate everything about us we may find the price of that skill is not only our authenticity, but a growing cynicism for new ideas. (Remember the three-step Graves or Harste's cycle? Have you cloned your author today?) When the poems are our own, shaped and kneaded and scratched from our own hand, they can be exchanged with others and we will all learn.

The bat-poet, by separating from the others, was able to write a poem that "has all the things we do." Only a bat could write that poem. John Carter, who says he cannot separate his professional development from his growth as a person, says he tries not "to feel constraints or be concerned about what others may feel, but to try to hold on to the philosophy of not following the path, and instead to go where there is no path and leave a trail."

> Professional renewal is an essential ingredient in good teaching that we can neither buy nor have bestowed upon us: we renew ourselves by revising who we are and what we do, daily and consciously, alone and together, with students, colleagues, and friends.

As we explore our professional change, we must remind one another that what we know about young readers and writers we know about all people learning, from six to gray-haired sixty: everyone has a right to have a say in their own learning, to write their own poems.

But as the bat-poet says: "The trouble isn't making poems, the trouble's finding someone to listen to them."

PROFESSIONAL RENEWAL IS AN ESSENTIAL INGREDIENT in good teaching that we can neither buy nor have bestowed upon us: we renew ourselves by revising who we are and what we do, daily and consciously, alone and together, with students, colleagues, and friends.

The bat-poet stayed awake when other bats slept, observed from a new spot, listened to the many voices and sounds that fellow bats preferred to ignore. When the bat-poet decided to write poetry about being a bat, to create poems of the bat experience, the material was abundant.

So, too, is material about our teaching. What poems can we create of our experience and who will listen to them? If we think of our professional behavior itself as poetry, what are the many ways in which we recreate ourselves, crafting new perspectives? What do these poets among us know?

THREE TEACHER-CONSULTANTS in Mississauga, Ontario schools, combined their professional commitment to growth, their friendship, and their classroom experience to work with teachers in the district. For many years Rosemary Buckley, Jeannette Schlatman, and Marilyn Cerar helped teachers prepare materials, organized and presented at small conferences, and shared a wealth of books and materials. What sets them apart from many who have similar jobs is that their approach to working with others transcends job demands. Rather than parachuting supplies into schools, these three offer teachers their boundless sense of humor, their affirming approach to growth, and their straight-on political sensibility.

Within the school district, but outside the schools, Earl Rutledge headed a Teacher's Center open evenings and weekends for professional use. To most observers, the small wooden building in Bridgewater, Nova Scotia that overlooks the river houses up-to-date computers, laminating and photocopying materials, books, articles, and graphic aids. But the tiny quarters hold more than materials; they house the spirit of the teaching enterprise itself. Earl's energetic approach to supporting teachers in their own learning made the center a professional home. Conversations that begin here—over the PCs or the film processing—bring teachers back again and again. Some of the teacher talk has spun the production of videotapes and curricular materials that are in demand across the continent.

The opportunities for professional renewal in institutions are endless. Teachers flock yearly to the New Hampshire writing program, for example, or to Mount Saint Vincent University's summer institute for teachers. But often the professional poetry teachers create in these settings is inspiration to continue their growth without benefit of the academy or the school district. Out of John Portelli's Philosophy for Children section of the summer institute, for example, grew a teacher group that met monthly for several years to discuss the ways they foster talk and critical reflection in their classrooms.

BEYOND THE REQUIREMENTS OF THEIR GRADUATE WORK at Indiana University, Kathy Egawa, Beth Berghoff, Carolyn Beverstock, and others, formed a teachers' ways of knowing group, a loose collective of teachers and graduate students that explored, in Kathy's words, "what makes teachers tick." Sensitive to the fact that they were (and are) teachers who are now part of the academic discourse community, this group determined to hear the voices of teachers at work, to hear their thoughts about the ways they see themselves as individuals and professionals. Group member Hester Hemmerling believes that the open inquiry the collective promoted gave teachers "a listening ear so they can articulate what they do and how, and then grow from that." (Egawa 1991)

Like the bat-poet, we know that it has been difficult to find a listening ear for our teaching stories. And yet, it seems that may be changing. Across North America, the renewed interest in narrative as a way of knowing continues to grow. Heartened by the wealth of research supporting narrative inquiry, teacher-led groups are gathering to talk about the patterns, the metaphors, and the rhythms that shape their life in teaching. Teachers telling stories of their experience is not new: what is new is educators' growing willingness to see narrative as a legitimate way in which we know. This shift, of course, is both exciting and profoundly disturbing. Telling teaching stories has always been an authentic means of professional growth—more so, I believe, than accepting intellectual supplies from outside sources—and yet, until the work of Grumet, Clandinin, Pinar and others began validating what most teachers instinctively knew, we tended not to take our own stories seriously.

> Teachers telling stories of their experience is not new: what is new is educators' growing willingness to see narrative as a legitimate way in which we know.

Weaving analysis and argument with story and theory in front of a fireplace became the tradition of the Camp Hilles collective, a group of teachers, consultants, professors, and students led by Gerry Carty and Allan Neilsen who initiated a weekend retreat twice a year in a remote estate at Canada's Annapolis Valley. Although the focus sometimes was community salad-building, finding firewood, or singing traditional Cape Breton songs late into the night, the ever-changing group set its agenda each time—evaluation, perhaps, or supporting change in their school district—and each meeting ended with a sense of renewal. Fusing laughter and conviction with the dressed-down talk that belongs around a country kitchen table, the individuals became a community and, paradoxically, enabled each to be just who he or she is.

THESE PROFESSIONAL ALLIANCES are everywhere: change the setting, the precise nature of the group, or the focus of the talk, and we can find such communities growing from Seattle to Texas to Hong Kong. Each of us knows of a writing group that provides support, or an after-school collective, or a staff that easily blends friendships with the demands of school change. These communities, the wellspring of the poetry of teaching, usually have no name, no yearly dues, and no duties except for one: to meet on their own terms for the benefit of individual and group. With no reason to proselytize or promote, such alliances can be professional homes where trust and tolerance meet, and to which we can always return.

TRUTH IN TEACHING

I REMEMBER THE TIME OUR SON JESSE TOLD A LIE. Noticing an angry red mark on his wrist, I asked him how it happened. He looked up, his eyes averting mine ever-so-slightly, "Daze bit me," he said.

"Dave bit you!"

"Yes. And Nonna too. Me say ouch!"

"And Donna bit you too? Well, that must have hurt quite a bit."

"Yes. Me sad."

I had a hard time concealing my broad smile. This was not only the most outrageous fib Jesse had ever told, it was also the most fluent conversation we had ever had in his four years of life. The red mark, it seems, had been caused by wet wool mittens chafing his wrist. And as far as we could tell, Donna and Dave, his middle-aged friends, confined their biting to the dinner table.

As parents of a child whose struggles with language have kept us on edge, we rejoiced in Jesse's emerging ability to shape a conversation. For years, he had used two-word sentences and unique sounds to communicate with us, and mostly for functional reasons. To hear him fluently construct a story of being bitten was cause not for alarm, but for joy. This story, like the truth in many a four-year-old's life, was the fish tale of a boy who is using language to revel in his imagination and pull his parents' leg in the process. What some would call a lie, I celebrated as part of a larger truth: the clear and welcome sound of our son's growth.

I heard a similar sound in the early mornings as our eldest son, David, sat at the piano, trying to perfect a simple, yet challenging tune. As other family members filled the toaster, lit the wood stove, and searched for a second mitten, David picked his way through the notes, repeating, hesitating, faltering. Occasionally, his practice earned him a musical breakaway, and the entire household seemed to pause. The song cut through our early morning fog like a sun ray, a perfect and yet fleeting balance of harmony, rhythm, and melody. David's fingers and determination shaped for him, if only briefly, a pure and clear sound, the morning's musical truth.

Moments of such harmony and purity are, for me, moments of truth. I realize I am walking into territory explored by poets and philosophers who are much better equipped for the journey than I am. But if truth can be an individual matter, as I believe it can be, then I will offer my impression of its meaning for our collective travels through learning and teaching. Because for me, next to being a parent, only one other experience grants me the opportunity to sense truth, and that is the educative experience.

Truth, for me, is a sentient, full-bodied notion. It's a jolt of genuine connection, something closer in fidelity to the experience and knowing at hand than a correspondence to what some may call "actual facts." Truth, as I want to describe it—and language cannot, will not, bring it to life for me here—is not the truth we know as a generalized proposition, for in our efforts to translate it beyond the moment, it dies. Nor is it a statement of reckoning, a victory of right over wrong, or the mere opposite of a lie. The truth I struggle to write about here is more like yeast than bread, more like a watercolor wash drying on ever-changing images than a portrait displayed, more like fresh air of the soul than words on the page. It is hard won, ephemeral, and as Oscar Wilde said, rarely pure, and never simple.

> The truth I struggle to write about here is more like yeast than bread, more like a watercolor wash drying on ever-changing images than a portrait displayed, more like fresh air of the soul than words on the page.

With this sense of truth before me, I want to examine our search for it in education. This is a recurrent theme in my writing, and I come back to it, I believe, because our deeply held notions of truth and right and wrong in teaching are so pervasive and so entrenched that they continue to appear daily even in the most casual of conversations. What disturbs me is not our quest, but the ease with which we abandon it.

As educators, we have traditionally looked outside ourselves for the answers to our pedagogical questions. Because education is a mosaic of disciplines, we rarely accord ourselves a professional respect equal to our responsibility. We are "just teachers," and because each of us is part of a larger bureaucratic structure, we tend to have neither the opportunity nor the inclination to make all our own curricular decisions. Practically, we argue, we couldn't do it: too much goes into the making of the school experience to decide everything for ourselves. Attempting to orchestrate daily the often relentlessly chaotic activities of busy children leaves us little time for reflection, let alone decision making. Time, the school's primary mechanism of control, is seldom in our hands. As a result, when we are struck by an unease about what we are doing, are challenged by a uniquely troublesome learner, or feel uninformed or powerless (which can be often), we want the benefit of others' knowledge or experience, a borrowed truth, the wisdom of a colleague, or the promise of valid research.

And it is part of the educational research tradition to supply these so-called truths, these ways of knowing and doing. In literacy education, we consume and have been consumed by standards of rationality that include consistency, economy, coherence, and above all, generality. The scientism that has controlled research in literacy has demanded, for teachers and for researchers, what Suzanne

Langer has called "maximal interpretability." This means that knowledge, presented in propositions, is tested by observable fact. When the proposition and the facts correspond in the largest number of circumstances, a "truth" is born. As Langer claims, each generation seeks truth, and whatever will guarantee the truth of propositions to its satisfaction, is where thought comes to rest in knowledge.

But propositions, of course, are stated in language, both the means and end (if there is one) of literacy education. We take the written word seriously because it is our mandate to do so. But, as Eisner (1988) reminds us, propositional discourse, by its very nature, generalizes more than it particularizes; that is, we want to search for and claim a truth about readers in general, rather than a reader in particular. This dominance of propositions, as Eisner calls it, has remained relatively unchallenged for decades. The creators and caretakers of the governing truths in literacy education have often been academics who send out assistants to retrieve the necessary facts from the front lines. Publishers of reading series and teaching aids buy the researcher's name and his current truth to produce "knowledge" in consumable form, a way to feed teachers who are starved for time, and school boards who long for standards and conformity. Here is where thought, the collective thinking apparently supported by research, comes to rest in something we then claim as knowledge.

But recently the point where thought comes to rest in knowledge is shifting, becoming more slippery to define. While no one can deny that some educational research has provided us with useful generalizations, the cost of these marketable "truths" has been too high. More than just the intellectual price of deskilled teachers who "teach from the book" (although that, in itself, is cause for alarm), our willingness to rely on truths created outside our experience has cost us the heart and soul of our profession, our belief in ourselves.

> ...our willingness to rely on truths created outside our experience has cost us the heart and soul of our profession, our belief in ourselves.

But I am confusing two issues here. One is the process by which information or contemporary thinking is transformed into knowledge. The other is how we receive this knowl-edge, and what we do with it. Let's deal first with the process of creating knowledge.

To move away from the influence of the church as the font of wisdom and truth, thinkers in the nineteenth century embraced the notion of empiricism: proof by the collection of sense data, observable "fact." Science replaced religious doctrine as the provider of knowledge. But empiricism has been used badly. One of the preoccupations of the 1800s was the study of craniology, prompted by the colonial interest in determining which sex and which race was superior in intelligence.[1] A variety of methods were used to determine that men of color, and all women, were inferior in intelligence, predicated on the obvious assumption that brain size was equated to intelligence.

1. For further information about the study of craniology, especially with regard to its political misuses, see the work of Elizabeth Fee.

Scientists adjusted their methods with each challenge to the proof at hand: elephants, for example, could not be seen to have greater intelligence than people. And using cranial size relative to body size would reveal women's brains to be larger. Perhaps then it was a particular part of the brain that held intelligence; this notion prompted further research that would reveal indisputably the superior intelligence of Caucasian males.

Research truths, regardless of the century, have been notorious for the way in which they dovetail with conventional wisdom, with the political will of the time.

A more recent example is the case of the gay Florida dentist, David Acker; six of his patients contracted AIDS and brought suit against him. The Centers for Disease Control (CDC) in Atlanta took statements from the patients about their risk factors and had the individuals undergo a variety of tests, then compared the strain of HIV Acker carried with the strains carried by at least one of the patients, a young woman who claimed no sexual activity at all. The CDC concluded, because of the similarity of the strains, and the seeming absence of other risk factors, that the patients' contact with Acker was the most likely cause of their HIV infection. This conclusion translated to a new, rapidly spreading assertion, the medical equivalent of a truth: HIV can be transmitted by your dentist.

The devastation to Acker's career and the resulting panic in the public could not be overturned. Now, years later, it has come to light that each of these individuals had other, very obvious risk factors that likely contributed to their contracting the virus. But until this information travels throughout the media and the health care system with the weight and speed of the earlier, more accepted "truth,"—and of course it never does—most people will think otherwise.

The point here is not to decide if we can or cannot contract HIV from a health care professional. Obviously and unfortunately, that remains to be seen. The point is that conventional fears and conventional wisdom can cloud the "scientific" search for truth. The process of scientific inquiry is not, and has never been, free from political and economic agendas. Few studies done in the name of "objective" science are possible, given the strength of political and economic will to prove otherwise. Studies of the negative effects of tobacco, for example, were hidden from the public for decades. Even now, some of the most expensive research done on the effects of tobacco is funded by, you guessed it, the tobacco companies.

The medical profession, even more than the field of education, is vulnerable to political and economic influence. And the medical stories are the ones we are most likely to hear about on television or read in the newspapers. Hasn't each of us been exasperated at one time or another? Yesterday it was saturated fats that were the only villains, now hydrogenated fats are bad too. Will there be anything left to eat anymore?

Surely all these researchers aren't unethical, are they? Of course not. My point is that our science is a reflection of the spirit of the times. As a citizen of a threatened British empire, each of us, as distasteful as it is to imagine, may have been supportive of research that asserted the dominance of white males. We believe what we often need to believe. And, too often, so do scientists.

Education has operated its own assembly line of manufactured truths for many decades. In the days of the rise of behaviorism, almost every human act was reprocessed through the behaviorist "sausage machine." Teaching became the application of the right stimulus to prompt the organism to respond by learning. The point was to reinforce the appropriate behavior, and extinguish the inappropriate. Reading then, became thought of as a primarily stimulus-response activity. The resulting studies, which talk of children in terms not far from Pavlov's dogs, are often comical to review.

The influence of phenomenology and hermeneutics gave rise in the 1980s to the notion of constructivism. Readers, as Jerry Harste has often said, do not bark at print, they build meaning by interacting with the words on the page. Their prior knowledge, combined with the material at hand, shapes a "new knowledge," a meaning unique to the reader. Extremists of this view of reading asserted that no shared meaning can exist in a text, that each encounter with text is irrevocably individual.

The game of either-or continued with the process-product, whole language versus skills debate. When researchers such as Lisa Delpit entered the fray to caution that perhaps skill and drill was not as dangerous to the development of black children's literacy as current wisdom would make it, and perhaps instead could be empowering because of the children's then greater access to the discourses of power—the movement was, for an academic moment, somewhat subdued.

The second issue, how we receive knowledge and what we do with it, comes into play here. The "knowledge machine," like the sausage machine I referred to earlier, will chug along regardless of what we do in our classrooms. (I am reminded of Donald Murray's insightful comment: you cannot infer the pig from the sausage).

What is important is that we accept received knowledge as, first of all, provisional. Truth is fleeting because, like the planet and all we do on it, truth cannot stand still. Writer Ursula Le Guin talks about truth as a sense she has when she is engaged in the art of tai chi. Each movement is purposeful and balanced, and each leads to the next; it must, in order to maintain such balance. The stillness, the harmony, can only be realized by her constant and graceful movement from one position to another.

Our so-called scientific truths shift in this manner, and we must not forget that each position was right for its time. So too our individual or personal truths shift. These belief systems, our personal knowledge, are borne out of our own lifelong empiricist activities. As we live, we gather experience and observe carefully in the classroom and in the world. As we live, these accumulated experiences settle into truths, sometimes more sedimented than they ought to be for our own survival. A teacher who insists on maintaining a single-focused and tomblike quiet in a nineties classroom, for example, may be struggling so hard to maintain his belief in the truth of that practice for education that his efforts are focused solely on upholding it. In an age of vocal children accustomed to a life of multiplexing (doing more than one thing at once, particularly if it's technological), the truth—that a classroom that is quiet for six hours is the best place for learning—must necessarily be revised. If not, the balance in both teaching and learning, for the teacher and the students, is lost.

Does this mean we throw out all those truths that seem to have worked? Does this mean that nothing is anything anymore? Lest you think I would lead a movement into radical relativity and toss tradition or wisdom aside, I assure you I would not. But a fear of chaos, of wallowing in relativity is an either-or response to the suggestion that we accept truths provisionally. Accepting truth as a moving notion, a balance that is right for the time, does not mean that no truths exist. It simply means that truths, like people, have a life cycle, and a mo-

> ...truths, like people, have a life cycle, and a momentum.

mentum. Some are more or less robust than others; some more tenuous, others more enduring. We simply have to be aware: the truth can be as fleeting as my son's morning piano moment, or as enduring as our understanding that an affirming atmosphere is more beneficial to children than a punitive one (it took a century to get to that one), but it will never truly sit still.

Adrienne Rich's poem about truth reminds us that truth is like the pattern on the surface of the carpet. When we become weavers we see the tiny threads that create the pattern, and we also see the knots on the underside. The hope for education, I am convinced, lies in the spirit of the growing numbers of teachers who, like weavers, are examining their own practice and creating their own truths. And in the spirit of all teachers, whose daily dedication to other people's children weaves tapestries wider and more complex by the year, this hope is enough perhaps to warm a generation.

GARDENS

LAST YEAR, I PLANTED A GARDEN AGAIN. For years, the occupations that become life itself, such as raising children, teaching, and academic work, demanded all my cultivating and nurturing skills. But last spring was the year I returned to the soil. I bought peat moss, marked a circle of stones around a spot that had become overgrown with weeds, retrieved the hoe from the back of the shed, and determined to grow green things again.

Thoughts of the rocky, sandy Nova Scotia soil, however, the springtime clouds of rain and fog, the rabbits, the wanton dogs and the porcupines reminded me of what I was up against. This patch will never be like the flat, cultivated plots of rich, blackish loam I recall from my childhood in Western Canada. But standing by the side of the hill, trying to decide what to plant where, I was also reminded of how good it feels to have my hands in the earth, to work around visible growth, to watch and learn from the plants' daily progress just as I watch and learn from the faces of my children.

My garden looks out over St. Margaret's Bay, from which stretches the ocean beyond. When I am down on my haunches, with a fistful of weeds, digging out stones and swatting black flies from my neck, I can look out to the sea and the sky. To see beyond my garden means more to me than a satisfying view: it is an essential connection, a life-thread to gardens elsewhere on earth, a reminder that other workers on the planet hold a promise of growth in their hands with much less reason than me.

WE KNOW THAT, regardless of the measure we use, over 900 million adults in the world are illiterate and 95 percent of these people are from developing countries. What we don't stop to think about—or what we choose to ignore—is that the majority of those who cannot read or write and are denied access to schooling are women and female children. Broad-brushing our statistics the way we love to do allows us to talk in generalizations, to cluck with concern, and to turn back to our own gardens, thankful for our relative bounty.

> What I cannot seem to understand is how a profession rooted in nourishing the spirit of learning can be so isolating and lonely...

As teacher-gardeners, we are surrounded daily with the voices and hands of busy, growing bodies, and yet we often feel alone. Classrooms, the plots of mind and soul in which tending, watching, and cultivating ought to create perennial growth, often fail to provide the elements necessary to keep the gardener strong. What I cannot seem to understand is how a profession that is rooted in nourishing the spirit of learning can be so isolating and lonely; and how the enterprise that binds our efforts as professionals—promoting literacy for all—can keep millions of the world's nurturers in exile. I think these gardeners—teacher-gardeners and illiterate women—are connected, and I want to explore how.

A RURAL WOMAN IN THE DEVELOPING WORLD is typically pregnant and surrounded by young children. She does up to three-quarters of all agricultural work in addition to her daily domestic tasks, such as carrying jars of water long distances and finding food for her family (Chlebowska 1990). She is a faceless woman of color who, worldwide, provides two-thirds of the world's labor for one-tenth the pay, and whose efforts are excluded from calculations of national productivity (Eisler 1987). The expectations of her culture, the demands of her religion, and the social mores of her community keep this woman from owning property, having the access to schooling her brother has, making simple family decisions, indeed, even from eating before her husband is fed.

In Bangladesh, one in three girls is in school and 24 percent more women than men are illiterate. Elsewhere, the situation is worse: in oil-rich Saudi Arabia, fewer than 46 percent of girls are enrolled in primary or secondary schools; in the Yemen Arab Republic, 93 percent of Yemeni women are illiterate and only 15 percent of the primary school students are girls.

And yet. And yet. We know statistically and irrefutably that it is maternal education, not income, that is the greatest factor in reducing infant mortality. We know that literate mothers bear fewer children. Literate girls marry later and are more likely to break with cultural practices that threaten the family's health. A literate mother can read the label on a six-cent cure for a deadly water-borne disease and save her child's life. A literate mother can teach her own children, and can think beyond survival.

But our traditional economic systems, whether they are capitalist or communist, are built on the "alienation of caring labor" (Eisler 1987). Women's work doesn't count, at least not in calculations of national productivity or labor-force statistics. Unpaid work in the home and in the fields—bearing children, doing household chores, raising small livestock and handling food production—keeps women from attending literacy programs or gaining access to any form of schooling. This vicious cycle perpetuates illiteracy and poverty for millions of the world's female population. It's criminal, we think. It's too overwhelming to think about. But as I curse the stones that resist my garden spade, I curse not only the plight of a Kurdish woman on a hillside far beyond, or a Zimbabwe mother carrying jars of water from the river, I curse the fact that we continue to hide the female face of these problems. Illiteracy hits women the hardest. Access to power through education is a problem of gender inequity.

When the rights of women to read their world are denied, the rights of humans of both sexes are denied: both male and female children, struggling to survive in barren soil, lose the chance to lead healthy, productive, and rewarding lives.

TALKING ABOUT THE CLASSROOM AS A GARDEN is a cliché, I know, but I want to revive the metaphor by discussing it from a new perspective. Teachers are lonely gardeners for many reasons, not the least of which is the institutionalized alienation of our "caring labor" (to use Eisler's words again). Although the threads seem to be tenuous, teachers are connected in fundamental ways to illiterate women in faraway places. Both suffer intrusion from the power structures. As people who don't work the soil, don't know the feeling of earth through their fingers, presume to tell the gardener in a developing country what to plant and how to weed, water, sort, measure, and adjust the local environment to create a better, more productive garden, so research tanks, government bodies, and phalanxes of public policy makers decide about literacy education with little knowledge of the impact of such decisions on a classroom. So-called public interest groups threaten the intellectual freedom of students and teachers by denouncing particular teaching approaches or books at a time when the need for literacy for all is crucial. Researchers continue to spend time away from a garden, counting beans and sorting species, to

> When the rights of women to read their world are denied, the rights of humans of both sexes are denied.

come up with better measures to feed literacy education's competitive machine. Through tradition and by their own presumptions, these self-appointed Master Gardeners, comfortably ensconced in positions of power, deny or trivialize teachers' knowledge of their own gardens. Teachers' caring labor, their hard-won experience working the soil, is rarely considered in calculations of educational productivity. It certainly is not considered when large-scale policy decisions are made. Teaching is largely women's work—in the Western world women comprise two-thirds of the teaching population in comparison to almost 90 percent worldwide—and women's work doesn't always count. In familiar gardens, too, access to power through education is a problem of gender inequity.

> When the right to make professional decisions...is denied, the human right to intellectual and academic freedom is denied as well.

When the right to make professional decisions—how to inform practice or what to choose as reading material—is denied, the human right to intellectual and academic freedom is denied as well. The denial needn't be blatant, through policy or law: it is usually enough to use salary and promotion practices, extra-curricular responsibilities, and the assessment carrot (or stick, depending on your view) to keep the scales unbalanced. Sometimes it takes less: a teacher who submitted a written account of her changing thoughts on evaluation to her district office as a discussion paper had the paper returned to her with red-penned edits. Another, who kept a teaching log to inform her teaching, was required to gain district approval to undertake research in her classroom.

Am I angry? Yes. Naive? No, not if the charge of naiveté is someone's way of persuading me to accept the status quo. The problem is not simply men, nor is it women, if we think only in terms of genetic make up. The problem uniting powerless teachers in Western societies and illiterate women in the developing nations is a problem of the imbalance of two views of the world.[1] Eisler talks about two models: one based on competition and hierarchies, with one group being superior to another and usually by force. In this model, patriarchy and matriarchy are legitimate terms because they represent either male dominance or female dominance. The conqueror, most often male, but sometimes female, carries the blade. The other model is a partnership model: here social relations are based on linking, not ranking, on cooperation and harmony. In this model, diversity does not mean inequity. It simply means difference.

Some say the impulse to dominate—whether it is in the house, in the marketplace, or in test scores—is a natural human impulse, male or female. I say it is also natural to

---

1. Obviously this argument is simplistic. Currently, however, with national borders being supplanted by transnational economic ones, we can still claim that the impulse to dominate economically maintains, and exacerbates, global divisions. Money is too often the bottom line, regardless of which page in life we refer to.

want harmony and cooperation, to give ear and voice and word to everyone who tends the garden and knows the earth from which it grows. The gardens, after all, in education and the global economy, are getting larger and their boundaries are blurring. Maybe it is time we gave the responsibility for shaping their future to those who take the time to care for them.

A DANCE OF THE HEART,
A SONG OF THE SOUL

A CULTURE IS A PLACE FOR GROWING THINGS, I read once. What does the school culture grow? As I emptied my son's schoolbag, my heart sank. A Father's Day card-in-progress (he had obviously not finished it in time), there were mimeographed cut-outs of a hammer and other tools, a brass spread pin for attaching these items so they could rotate on the page, and fill-in-the-colors lettering. I wondered what he thought of this task, for certainly it looked like a task. I knew what I thought of it.

As a former art teacher, I recall the days of chaos in junior high when pimple-faced man-boys focused their random energy on a large lump of clay, pounding out the air bubbles, shaping it, pushing it, and only occasionally giving in to the impulse to throw a wet clump at a smart-aleck classmate. I recall the year of the mask, when each of these motorcycle-driving miscreants, late or absent in other subjects, insisted on showing up to art class to lie prostrate on the table, breathing only through a straw, while others shaped plaster to the contours of their faces. The Vaseline, the plaster, the wraps, the molds, and the mess became, for this all-male class, an event, like a rock concert: anybody who was anybody was there, bragged about it, held the finished product triumphantly in their hands to the cheers of the others.

These were the days before the Phantom, but at the peak of popularity of rock icons such as Gene Simmons of Kiss; yet I believe that the pop culture influence did not resonate as strongly in the sensibility of those adolescent boys as did other, deeper needs. They wanted to work at the edge of confusion and new possibilities, to extend beyond the paper and words that had dominated and alienated them for a decade. They wanted to be able to muck about, and to get approval for it. Like the Lost Boys, they also wanted a sense of communal purpose, and a home. And they wanted to create something with their own hands, the same hands that gripped an open book at an incomprehensible page for minutes at a time, that only rarely, and awkwardly, formed words on the page.

A blank white page and paints and markers became the media for my son's Father's Day card that year. I quietly put the mimeographed scraps in the garbage, and my son never asked about their whereabouts. The gender message the card sent was enough to push several of my buttons, but even more disheartening to me were the messages such a

"creation" gives to a child, about giving, and about creating. I am a parent who loves nothing more than an original
drawing or poem, a bouquet of handpicked wildflowers, or
a homemade meal as a gift. Why buy, I always think, when
we have so much, as the fruit of our own hands and hearts,
to offer? A third-hand card says to a child my own words are
not enough, my own drawing is not enough, my own
ingenuity pales against a craft pattern that can make a tool
handle rotate on the page. Giving is a sacred act, as is
creating; what are we telling children when we encourage
gift giving that denies the self in the event? Certainly I have
received store-bought gifts, and loved them, but that is not
my point. The first lesson we teach ought to be that of
creating, to help shape the self, and, in so doing, how then
to give it.

As teachers of literacy, we hope to guide students
into reading not only the word, but the world, as Paulo
Freire has said. We have to remind ourselves, however, that
we read the world in many ways, using many sign systems,
multiple media. A teacher of language is more than a
teacher of words, or she ought to be. Language, beyond the
conventional understanding of different tongues—French,
Ukrainian, English, Portuguese, and the like—is a mode of
expression to create meaning, to communicate, to stir the
intellect, the emotion, and the soul. I can stand before the
room-sized art work of Laurie Walker in Montreal and
find no words to take away to explain to you what I saw. I
only feel, and the worm of disruption that wiggles in my
psyche after having seen the sculpture continues to play

havoc with my conventional sense of things. The sculpture has a language, but the language is not in words.

Jesse's trademark drawings of houses with beanstalks, each magical in its use of primary colors, tell in another way. Another child moves, performs as she talks, acting out her story as naturally as breathing. Still another sings, creates songs, picks out tunes on the piano, and writes her own words. The signs, the other ways of expression, are there, and the children use them. But do we, as teachers, read them, help them to thrive in the culture we create at school?

IN THE LAST TWO YEARS ALONE, our school districts have not only lost physical education and resource teachers, they have lost their music, art, and drama consultants and teachers at all levels except senior high, where a small corps of arts teachers remain to ensure a "balanced" curriculum. Our situation is not uncommon; as you read this, you will be able to echo your own cutback horror story. Economic exigencies have demanded that schools focus only on core areas, that schools excise the extras, subtract the add-ons. The dollar defines what our priorities will be, say the policy makers. But we know that argument is backward: as in all economic systems, our spending is a reflection of our values.

And so we find ways to live with the consequences of a curriculum with its heart cut out. For that is what has happened, I believe. When we take "arts" out of the language arts, and leave only reading and writing words on the page, we take the heart out of learning, the soul out of the curriculum. When we teach notes without singing, and movement without dancing, when we teach about playwrights without performing, and colors without painting, we are left with a lifeless classroom.

We have tin men without hearts directing educational agenda, and our schools will produce tin men and women as a result. But what is this heart we are missing? Why ought we to include arts in the language arts, broader literacies in our understanding of reading and writing? Here are three among dozens of reasons:

> We have tin men without hearts directing educational agenda, and our schools will produce tin men and women as a result.

+ We are many ways human, and many ways intelligent as Howard Gardner's foundational work on multiple intelligences has shown. Schools value and foster two intelligences: linguistic intelligence (having to do with words) and logical-mathematical intelligence (understanding numbers and their operations), and leave the others to wither. Indeed, many children fall into the educational cracks because their way of knowing and of communicating is neither recognized nor given room in the classroom. (In fact, there is a whole school of thought that believes that most so-called "learning disabled" and "at risk" children are simply children in this category. Who among us has not heard of the Down's syndrome child who can play Mozart, the adolescent non-reader who creates breathtakingly powerful drawings or videos with strong, intelligent messages?)

The other intelligences Gardner has observed (and around which he has founded a school and research center

in Cambridge) include bodily-kinesthetic, musical, intraper-
sonal (self), interpersonal (social), and spatial-visual. Gardner
claims that the arts represent all intelligences and to fail to
foster growth in each of these areas is to fail our responsibility for developing all cognitive domains. We construct
meaning in a number of ways, and the development of
concepts in one domain enhances the learning of concepts
in another. A tin man who considers the study of arts as a
frill might be reminded that the College Entrance Exami-
nation Board noted SAT scores 34 points higher in verbal
and 18 points higher in math sections for students who had
four years of music and arts compared to those who had
only one year. (To resort to arguing in the tin man's terms
seems reprehensible, but it may be what needs to be done.)
More powerful an argument I believe must be our commitment to teach a whole person, not one intellectual limb.

✦ Teaching the arts in schools helps to promote the
idea that we are actors in life, not spectators. It teaches a
fundamental sense of agency. In the same way "process"
learning and whole language philosophy argue for motivation to come from the child's purposeful and meaningful
choices in reading and writing, the arts promote the primacy of self representation in a social context. We are
always in the process of becoming, and we nudge our
becoming as we work and learn with others. We do. We act.
We continue to become. An education in the arts requires
students to use their imagination, not the questions of a
textbook, and to use their own media, not the prescribed
ones for the activity at hand. As well, the arts in the

curriculum (as an integral part, not as an add-on) create greater opportunities for students to work with one another, to share insights, collect opinions and suggestions, extend ideas by bouncing them off the responses of others.

Anyone who has ever watched children build a snow fort or an indoor camp knows the focus, the concentration, and the time they will spend on the project. The decision making, the negotiation, the clever uses for hand-me-down items, the creation of a world unto themselves, all are active, self-directed activities, made more enjoyable by sharing the making with friends. And the learning becomes more than how to cut a chunk of snow without it breaking, more than the limits of snow as a material for construction. It includes learning self-discipline, restraint, cooperation, seeing the whole in relation to the parts, building dreams with our hands and then changing them as we need to. I can do that, says the child. I made, painted, sewed, carved, moved these things into new shapes and in so doing, the child learns, I can move my world.

✦ Teaching the arts teaches the joy and the process of creating. Whether or not there is a product at the end of the process is often irrelevant. It is important that all of us, but especially children, take the materials around us and play with them in new ways, going beyond the conventional sense of things. We need aesthetic experiences as integral parts of our lives, to deepen our lives and to extend the self.

When I paint or draw, I become absorbed. An hour can pass without my realizing. I find myself bringing the glass for the brushes to my lips instead of my coffee cup, so deeply am I into the page. Nothing can replace the sense of accomplishment of just the right shading in that spot, even if the rest of the drawing is not what I hoped. Nothing can describe the serenity of that meditative state we fall into when we are creating something with our hands, our bodies, our senses. Singers talk of the same experience, as do actors; but we need not be self-described painters or actors or singers in order to benefit from the process of creating. It is an essential human need, having nothing to do with ability or skill and everything to do with being human.

Researchers have found that schools in which the arts are integrated into the curriculum have an optimistic and energetic feel about them. Self-esteem and self-confidence rise, particularly with those formerly considered "at risk" students. There is a purposefulness to these schools, a sense of community, a pride in achievement.[1]

CAN WE, AS CLASSROOM TEACHERS AND ADMINISTRATORS, do anything about the impoverished state of the arts in schools? Of course we can. We can lobby for a return of the specialists, as a start. Well-educated and talented arts professionals need to populate our schools, like a maverick flower bursting through a crack in the sidewalk, to provide a presence of hope and possibility. These professionals bring us life and a fresh perspective. They also bring us courage. For these arts specialists, I am certain, although they want employment as much as the next person, would

---

1. See the February 1994 edition of the *Phi Delta Kappan* (available in most campus libraries), which is devoted to the arts in education.

argue that the courage shown by everyone to make the arts an integral part of our curriculum is as great, or greater, a need than having professionals overseeing such activity.

Heather Horsfall, formerly an arts teacher in Halifax, has recently found herself in administration. As a classroom teacher for many years, Heather made performance art and the visual arts an everyday event. She brought the arts out of the classroom into the school and into the street. Her students, some of whom had a strong history of failure in the conventional school system, thrived in the arts. One girl showed a surprising talent for speaking in public, another for organizing large and public events. Heather now makes the arts an integral part of the school where she is currently principal. The children, delighted with the chance she offered to organize the "course of their dreams," designed their own curriculum for a part of the year, providing work in mime, horseback riding, sculpture, video production, scuba diving, and other non-school activities. Even better, Heather gained the full support of the urban parents who saw this opportunity as enrichment for their children.

> ...we owe it to our students to provide them with an environment that is rich in imagination, play, risk, and adventure.

Speaking to teachers in my courses, Heather reminds us all that regardless of our own ability or experience in the arts, we owe it to our students to provide them with an environment that is rich in imagination, play, risk, and adventure.

But why don't we take up this offer? What is preventing us from going beyond agreement to action? Two forces hold us back, I believe. One is the school structure, "the system," if you will. And the other force, the more potent one, is of course, ourselves.

Schools bow to the gods of Efficiency and Control. To achieve those ends, curricula are segmented, compartmentalized, offered, and tested in bite-sized pieces. The pattern is linear. The hierarchy goes from top to bottom, the printing goes from left to right. Nothing provokes the ire of the gods more than activity that is random, circular, centripetal, recursive, that flouts the clock, causes large enthusiastic movement, and tosses material around. How can you control that? How can you measure it, test it, reproduce it?

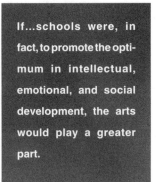

If...schools were, in fact, to promote the optimum in intellectual, emotional, and social development, the arts would play a greater part.

You can't, of course. And, as I mentioned earlier, it all goes back to what school systems value, what they believe their purpose is. If the purpose of schools were, in fact, to promote the optimum in intellectual, emotional, and social development, the arts would play a greater part. But the purpose of schools, in spite of what the latest mission statement says, is to socialize children. I distinguish here between fostering social development, which connotes learning how to work within community, and socialization, which connotes learning conformity, compliance, routine, gender role placement, class and ability placement, and deference to authority.

But we are the schools, folks. We all remember what Pogo said about the enemy: It is us. I bite my lip in frustration as the tempera paint spreads underneath the newspaper on the kitchen table and drips on the floor, but my child's resulting painting, a time away from the television or the Nintendo, is worth the mess. I wince at the dramatic gestures and the last row voice of my adolescent son in a stage no larger than the kitchen alcove, but his larger than life behavior is self-confident, poised, and witty, the result of years of performance art and drama school. During moments of impatience, I remind myself that a clean, quiet kitchen is too great a price for my children's well-being.

Classroom teaching is frenetic enough as it is, we can argue, without introducing disruptive activity. But even that argument holds no more water than a paper cup. Children given regular opportunity to create learn the discipline of self-imposed order soon enough: their creations depend on it. They learn respect for property, theirs and others, they learn timing and balance. They seek quiet when they need it, and closure when they need it. They learn to follow the rhythms and cycles of their aesthetic growth, and not the schedules imposed on them by others.

But the roadblocks we place in front of us, especially the misguided emphasis on efficiency and control, can be overcome to a degree. What is more difficult to overcome is our misguided belief in perfection, in the talent and skill of artists. I can't teach art, the argument goes, I can't even draw a straight line. Oh, I wouldn't even attempt performance art; how would I know if what they were doing was any good?

The same teachers who see the development of math awareness as a process, who understand that not all girls and boys aim to be mathematicians when they are adults, believe that art-making belongs to the talented, the students whose drawing looks most lifelike, whose musical skill surpasses all others in the classroom. It is a measure of how we separate art-making and the arts from our lives. It is also a measure of how we deny seeing it in ourselves.

> ...the albatross of expertness we, as teachers, carry on our necks: I cannot teach anything unless I know it cold. This...is not modesty or selfconsciousness...it is an adopted arrogance, a false belief in the role of the teacher as superior.

One part of that is the albatross of expertness we, as teachers, carry on our necks: I cannot teach anything unless I know it cold. This, of course, is rooted in our fear of being wrong, of risking exposure, of letting students see us learn along with them. It is not modesty or self-consciousness, as it appears on the surface to be: it is an adopted arrogance, a false belief in the role of the teacher as superior. If we revealed the modesty that made us teachers, the same modesty the great teachers of the world reveal, we would be teaching by learning, publicly and without apology.

We are all artists, in one form or another. We make artistic decisions when we arrange flowers or the furniture, when we dress, when we set the sights for a photograph or the table for a festive dinner. Even making a salad can be an art: the right combination of colors, textures, and flavors displayed in a way that pleases the eye, is an art-making event. But we prefer to hide artists in galleries, and name only the children with an abundance of ready-made talent the artists in our schools. Artists then remain people whose work appears in books or shows in urban centers, and who become accessible only by special visits to schools or by offering their talents to teach on a Saturday morning.

Tomorrow morning is a good time to start. A mural on that bare wall by the principal's office would be nice. Tempera renderings or skits of the characters in that Katherine Paterson book would draw a few more into the reading. A performance newspaper for the school—now that would be fun. Or a video—some parent will be willing to loan us a camera. What if we created songs out of that information they have been researching?

Imagine the possibilities. Children can. And we must find the heart to join them.

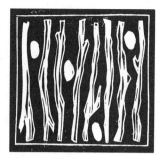

STICKS AND STONES

YOU ARE A STUDENT OF LIFE, invited to a master's garden for tea. As you sit at the table, he pulls out a stick and warns: "If you drink this tea, I will hit you with this stick. If you don't drink this tea, I will hit you with this stick." What do you do?

Posing this old problem always provokes a flood of responses, most of which are a variation on these: "I'd hit him first." Or, "I'd drink the tea. I might as well if I'm going to be hit anyway." Just as often: "I'd run away." The wisest solution, apparently, is also the simplest: Take the stick away.

This logic is familiar to teachers, parents and divorce lawyers who, to avoid endless arguments about toys or other belongings, practice Solomon-like wisdom and take the object away. It's not that easy, however, if words are the stick. It's even harder when we don't recognize them as such.

Words and people define our profession. We can also argue that our profession defines words and people. The chicken-or-egg thought and language debate is not just a koan for first year linguistics or philosophy, however; it is the key to our critical reading of texts and people. From our mouths or from the page, words are sticks: instruments of propaganda, indoctrination, and control.

As literacy educators, we claim to know this. But how often do we use this critical awareness reflexively?

As I read a recent magazine article by Lee Iacocca, my critical reading cap happened to be in full and locked position, allowing me to appreciate just how deft with words Chrysler's former leader can be. The stick he held was familiar.

"Teaching ought to be at the top of our list of professions, but it won't be as long as it remains a part-time job," Iacocca says (1990: 32). Mr. Iacocca claims the problem is that schools fail to put customer satisfaction first.

> "When a customer tells me that her car is terrific, I call the engineers and the manufacturing people and say 'don't change a thing.' But if the customer tells me the car is a lemon, I get my people working overtime to find out why and fix it." Lee suggests that overtime—increasing the school year from 180 to 240 days a year to compete with the Japanese model—would mean "more time for teaching, for special help when needed, and for a better evaluation of the product coming out...If I ran my factories half-time, I'd go broke" (Ibid.: 31).

I rolled my eyes, snorted, and threw the magazine aside. More teacher-bashing, I thought. More sticks raised against an already-bruised profession. Then I wondered how many of us would react just this way and decided to pick up the magazine again. The public's favorite gibes were all there. Teaching as part-time job: Don't we hear this at every social gathering from those-who-could-teach-blindfolded? Three months' vacation a year, early dismissal, paid-to-cut-Valentines, and so on. This perception, to Lee's credit as market mind-reader, is widely shared.

I reacted on cue to the remaining volleys. School-as-factory. The public as consumer; the student as product. Schooling to win a global competition (The Japanese are coming! The Japanese are coming!). The comfortable industrial, mechanical model. Education to take one's place on the main highway, and so on, and so on. (Students and schools as lemons, however, was a new—dare I say it?—twist.)

Lee raised all the sticks, pushed all our buttons. And, like the professional I claim to be, I started to marshal my scholarly arguments. The movie in my mind saw me facing Lee, across his large clean desk, with a sheaf of research reports in my hand.

I lay down the arguments like trump cards, one by one. Applying the industrial metaphor to education, especially literacy education, has resulted in widespread alienation, inequality, and intellectual and spiritual impoverishment. Freire (1970) chimed in: we persist (and we let others persist) in thinking of education as banking deposits of cultural capital. Literacy education is traditionally seen as the mechanistic transmission of consumable skills— taking, not making, knowledge. Publishers, capitalizing on the appetite this metaphor creates, produce homogeneous, assembly-line products, and de-skill teachers. Further, they worsen the gender bias in education, because assembly-line teaching takes away what few decisions women have in the profession. Using management models for tighter controls increases bureaucracy and segmentation, and exacerbates the problem (McNeil 1988). Valuing competition over cooperation will result in severe threats to our global survival (Franklin, 1990). And so on, and so on.

As the chorus of challengers to Lee's words grew larger, I thought again of his opening shot: "teaching ought to be at the top of our list of professions" and told the group to return to the reference section. We weren't going to take this stick away, I realized. Why? It's simple: because we carry it ourselves.

> In spite of what we know to be true...we, more than our critics, continue to buy and sell the consumer model of education.

In spite of what we know to be true, in spite of all the growth in our profession toward democratic practice, we, more than our critics, continue to buy and sell the consumer model of education. We'd like to think otherwise but, unwitting or not, we promote (and allow) the stick of industrialism and competition to define us. Although we are accepting the challenge of change in greater numbers, creating a collective sensibility marked by critical awareness, we still have a long way to go. We need to work harder—not, as Iacocca says, for customer satisfaction—but for defending what we claim to believe and making our actions consistent with those beliefs. In other words, we have to satisfy ourselves that we know what we stand for and take on our critics. (It's just about now that we sigh, toss the magazine down, walk away, enter our classrooms, look to the children, and close our door. But it's now, especially now, when it is most dangerous to do so.)

As a profession, we will always have richly diverse voices, varying perspectives, and conflicting views. To grow, we need them. But it's not consensus on the little things we need, it's just agreement in principle on the big ones. That's where Lee and his happy wagon-makers have it all over us; they know, at least, what their bottom line is: they stand for profit. And customer satisfaction is the most direct route to that bottom line.

So what about us? What is our bottom line as a profession and how do our actions and words reflect it? And how do we get there?

We could haul out all the usual shibboleths here: we stand for literacy for all, literacy for a critical and reflective citizenry, reading and writing to promote a strong democratic society. We know these and mouth them on cue. But we need to look in our own classrooms, our own districts, our assessment practices, our fix-a-broken-reader, teacher-as-lemon attitudes. We need to look in the mirror. We can start by looking at a resolution passed by the professional organization that represents nearly 87,000 reading educators, including you and me.

"Resolved that the International Reading Association affirm that reading assessments reflect recent advances in the understanding of the reading process; be it further

Resolved that assessment measures defining reading as a sequence of discrete skills be discouraged and that the International Reading Association opposes the proliferation of school by school, district by district, state by state, and province by province comparison assessments" (*Reading Today* Vol. 7, No. 5 (April/May 1990): 2).

Now let's look at three ads from a recent annual convention program (published about the same time), the advertising from which helps to finance production of the booklet and of our annual professional gathering. These ads suggest that while our organization discourages assessing discrete skills, we are not averse to promoting the teaching of them.

"Reading is a skill...And proficient readers don't usually develop without training and practice in the fundamental skills. Students need to learn to read before they can read to learn."

"A great new way to combine phonics, reading, writing, and thinking...delight your students as they put decoding, vocabulary, and critical thinking skills to work solving riddles which focus on specific phonetic elements."

"A newly developed teacher's guide completes the
package. A skills matrix gives you quick access to the
specific areas of instructional emphasis your students need."

And from an earlier convention program, one of the major
advertisers' full color ads: "Students move easily from the
known to the new in a natural progression that shows clearly
what the skill is, why it's important, and how it's used."

If, at the most fundamental level, our professional
resolutions and our public face don't match, or these
resolutions bend easily to economic expediency, then what
do we stand for?

Lortie (1975: 80) talks about teachers' struggles with
professional status.

"An occupation is recognized as a profession in part
because people believe that its members jointly
possess arcane knowledge on matters of vital public
concern; when that belief is held by key decision-
makers like legislators, judges, and state officials,
they take action to avoid whatever dangers may lie in
permitting noninitiates to practice the trade...[but]
those charged with surveillance of [education's]
affairs do not believe that they require teacher participation."

Teachers, the kinder and gentler professionals, seem willing to let others define us, articulate who we are, regulate
us, buy us, sell us, and consume us: we are willing to let

government and business interests hold up any stick at all, and then we either use it on ourselves or walk away with a sigh because, well, they just don't understand. And besides, the public pays us; we have to be the ultimate public servant, don't we?

To continue the story of the stick and the tea party: Let's assume, for the sake of discussion, that the stick having the greatest potential to harm us is not the damned-if-we-do-or-don't industrial model, but our reluctance to make our stated beliefs and our actions consonant. Closing our individual classroom doors and playing it safe will undermine our professional integrity. Blaming others is the cowardly bureaucrat's route. Responding to every challenge (including this one) with "Ya, but…" doesn't move the profession forward or silence the public or our own doubts. (Worse, "Ya-but" is a bad model for demonstrating to students the critical literacy we claim to value. Critical literacy, as the saying goes, is as much caught as taught.)

Let's enter the conversation and take control of the words used against us by taking control of what we claim to believe. In the process of defining a profession, we will demonstrate something of worth to students. And next time we're invited to tea with the public, we can relax and enjoy it—as professionals.

PROFESSIONAL
CONVERSATIONS

"WHY IS THIS ARTICLE IN MY MAILBOX? Are you trying to tell me something about my teaching, or what?"

"Who's got time to read this foolishness?"

"This stuff is just common sense—I'm doing most of it already."

"So what's this? Are we supposed to drop the last trend and switch to this one?"

As part of our graduate reading seminar a few years ago, teachers such as Janice MacNeill started traveling conversation books. I suggested the book as a forum for reading, writing, and talking with other teachers, with administrators, students and parents. The books, three-ring binders or sheaves bound with large clips, quickly grew fat and dog-eared as teachers exchanged and responded to articles about literacy instruction, reported on interesting professional news, and wrote about their classroom stories, challenges, joys and frustrations. Occasionally, however, the response was not enthusiastic, as Janice and others discovered. When colleagues are challenged with new ideas in a journal article or at a staff meeting, their reactions, like those above, are not always positive.

> When colleagues are challenged with new ideas...their reactions, like those above, are not always positive.

The conversation books, like professional talk itself, require teachers such as Janice to break down barriers, to open the staff room or the classroom door to talk about beliefs and classroom practices. For many, such conversations among staff are not only rare, they are actively discouraged. At a time when professional renewal is changing the face of teaching, it is disheartening for those who have rekindled their energy not to be able to share their enthusiasm with their colleagues. (It's ironic, isn't it? Our work as teachers is to foster a lifelong love for learning, to make learning contagious. But it seems, like chicken pox, the virus is more acceptable in the young.)

Teachers who bring their new ideas and practices to the staff room conversation threaten to stir up a carefully-cultivated atmosphere of boredom and faded ideals. The enthusiastic are called "keeners," the "resident expert," or "ambitious." To be an apprentice to life and learning again, to mix the energy of a beginner with the wisdom of experience, can have the same effect on a staff as becoming a long distance runner in a community of couch potatoes: it just makes everyone else look bad.

But a professional community that resists new ideas is often one in which teachers feel besieged with responsibilities and frustrated in their attempts to effect change. They are overworked and tired, and the friend they once counted on for noon hour conversation has a newfound zest for teaching that they can't seem to share. The hardened cynic sneers at new ideas, and prefers to discuss the research he's done on buying a new car. The ones who went on automatic pilot years ago will continue to play cards or knit. And the one who has claimed the same chair for fifteen years and whose noon hour schedule can be ruined by a two-minute telephone interruption won't even hear the talk, let alone acknowledge it. Sometimes, as many teachers are learning, it's just easier to go back to the classroom and close the door.

> To be an apprentice to life and learning again, to mix the energy of a beginner with the wisdom of experience, can have the same effect on a staff as becoming a long distance runner in a community of couch potatoes: it just makes everyone else look bad.

But perhaps we don't have to. As one who has been called Pollyanna and has felt the chilly collegial climate myself, let me suggest a few ways that may help keep the door open to conversation and professional growth.

✦ *Admit You're Human.* Teachers have traditionally been charged with the responsibility for having all the answers in the classroom. Unfortunately, that weight of having to be right carries over into the staff room, where we rarely admit our mistakes, tell our embarrassing stories, or talk about what we see as failures in our practice. But telling such stories bridges more worlds than the appearance of perfection ever can. The classroom innovator who gives the appearance of "having arrived" (or, as one curriculum consultant was overheard saying, "being much farther along than the other teachers") can quickly become the staff pariah unless she or he is willing to admit to growing pains, mistakes, and false starts. When we reveal publicly what Brookfield (1990) calls the "critical incidents" in our teaching—those events or moments when we truly see ourselves in new, and often unsettling, ways—we are seen as fallible and (good heavens!) human.

And when we ask for another's opinion or help, and genuinely want to receive it, we are showing we have something to learn. Whether we approve of that teacher's reliance on worksheets, or her teaching of phonics in isolation, is not the issue for the moment: finding a common base for conversation is.

◆ *Remove the Label.* Literacy education is full of labels for students and teachers, markers that can create more camps than communities. In the last decade, anyone who is not a "whole language" or "process" teacher is apt to feel—or has been made to feel—like chopped liver. So, too, is anyone who doesn't claim to be a "learner." (Don't we all, in some way, learn every day?) Every label, regardless of how well-intentioned it may be, becomes a door that blocks thought and leaves someone outside. As children, we built playhouses, clubs with a name, and membership was always fun until the "we," the members, became "they," the outcasts. How often as professionals do we unwittingly play out that treacherous practice? How often does the label we choose judge more than it describes? I have heard special educators, high school teachers, and chapter one teachers cry out in frustration: "Stop labeling me. First and foremost, I am a teacher. I wish other teachers would remember that."

Using labels or trendy jargon can shut down a conversation as quickly as it began. So too can public displays or fanfare. If we wear the "risk-taking learner" role like the latest designer label, we may appear more like a copy than the real thing.

✦ *Walk Across the Room.* We tend to settle into groups, in the staff room or the cafeteria, and see things from that perspective. It's useful and healthy now and again to break camp and go into new territory. It takes a little courage to take the first step, especially if staff room patterns have years of tradition behind them, but the gesture can have a huge impact on the group as a whole. Taking a step sets others free, giving them confidence to do the same. And the room we cross, the boundaries we erase can be a classroom, a discipline, or an ideology. It's always easier, of course, to sit across the room and rationalize or pre-judge: "Oh, he wouldn't want to talk anyway." Or "Why bother. I know what her opinion is already." But the other side of a room, just like the other side of an idea, gives us a new perspective, and a broader one as well. We want students to break free, to try new ways and approaches: shouldn't we show that we can too?

✦ *Show, Don't Tell.* Nobody likes a know-it-all, especially if she or he teaches next to you. You know who they are: they're the ones who saw this in the Sixties, or who tried it and ditched it, or who read about it first. They're the ones with the last word, the proof, the zinger that shuts down the conversation. They'll tell you the straight goods on how to do just about anything, if you'd only listen. But we all know, in literacy learning, just as in marriage, parenting, or leadership, that demonstrations teach us more than words can ever say. And when we don't demonstrate what we advocate, our chances for a conversation based on trust go right out the window. In an educational climate, when everyone feels somewhat insecure, overworked, and assailed by rapid change, trust is essential to our professional well-being. We tend to trust those people who spend less time talking about their wealth of knowledge, and more time putting into practice what they believe.

✦ *Listen More, Talk Less.* Next to a Know-it-all, the Ya-but person is the next most irksome colleague. Each of us has been a Ya-but, but most of us do not stop to wonder why. Ya-but appears when we don't really listen to another's frustrations or stories; we are merely waiting with varying degrees of patience to tell our side, or to force our point. "Ya, I see what you mean, but I think…" "Ya, I know that, but…" Listening, genuinely asking for and hearing out someone's perspective on an issue, gives us a basis for trust, allows us to find threads from which we can weave conversations and professional relationships. Whether we are children or adults, we all have stories that need to be heard.

We provide space for students in our classes to speak; why do we assume that grown-ups do not need the same space that children do? Education is one profession in which its members are starved for adult conversation, for authentic human connections. It was the desire to make human connections that brought most of us into the field in the first place.

◆ *Learn to Recognize Fear and Frustration.* Often the people with the most brittle shell have the softest core, and if we can break through their hard exterior, we usually find an idealist with a larger than average heart. When I give workshops for teachers, I look for the one with his hands folded across his chest, the one with the glowering face, the one who strides in with guns ablazing and a smart retort for everything. This is usually the teacher who is most fearful of change and whose ideals are rusting into disillusion- ment. Given an opportunity to air their frustrations, even the most bitter of comments, in an open, non-threatening atmosphere does wonders for the group and for the crusty cynic. If we don't take the comments personally, but instead, empathize with the frustration and hear it out, we can move beyond confrontation to conversation.

Although we talk a lot about promoting collabora- tion, a sense of community, caring and responsiveness, education remains a field dominated by the need to win— to be seen as better, as having more, as knowing more. In fact, when we think of the many reasons why conversations among our colleagues don't flourish, we can probably trace the root cause to the most insidious educational virus of all, competition. Everyone needs to feel as though they are keeping up. When we aren't, like runners in a race, we get an injury, drop out, or make fun of the ones who enter. But races, as we know, aren't communities that endure.

And perhaps that's where our conversations ought to start: with a clear-eyed understanding of the roles we play in the communities of which we are a part. We talk about the many ways we want to create collaborative classroom environments, and we spend a great deal of time promoting them. But for those environments to thrive, they must be set in a larger context of a healthy professional climate. A classroom, just like the staff room, is part of the whole ecology. Closing our classroom door—at the school, district, college or university level—prevents the whole from functioning well.

BRINGING COLLEAGUES TOGETHER in a learning collective takes more genuine humility and strength than many of us have, but it may be essential for our students to see such a community at work. A literate person makes connections, stays open and flexible, and demonstrates tolerance and responsiveness. Our years of teaching have shown us that students learn those qualities as much by what they see and hear as by what they read and write. When our students peek into the staff room or overhear us in the hallway, they learn how adults work together. We owe it to them to show how professionals can work together for the benefit of everyone.

DEAR PARENTS:
PLEASE TAKE THESE TESTS

THREE-YEAR-OLD JESSE sits at the table with the speech pathologist. She shows him a series of pictures, and asks him to tell her the word for the person or object in the picture. Jesse's speech has been slow to develop since birth, but he has an active and inquisitive mind. She shows him a picture of a curb, and he remains silent. He stares at the next picture, a postman, unable or unwilling to answer. The specialist recommends treatment for Jesse.

What's wrong with this picture or, in Jesse's case, these pictures? Jesse lives in rural Nova Scotia where there are no sidewalks, and hence no curbs. His parents pick up their mail at the post office, where neither the male nor the female postal worker wears a uniform. None of Jesse's books have a picture of a curb or a postman. Except perhaps for television watching, what daily experiences does Jesse have that prepare him to do well on the items of this test?

Jesse is not alone. Millions of children are tested regularly in North America on skills or knowledge to which they have no access. Jesse is luckier than most; he lives in the white, middle-class culture that both serves and drives North America's huge testing machine. Merely living in that culture guarantees his survival. But children from different backgrounds and cultures are destined from birth to fail, and such tests help to ensure that will happen.

Why have standardized tests become so politically powerful in society? What educational myths do these tests promote? Do we have alternatives? What are the important questions we, as parents and teachers, ought to be asking here?

The first standardized test, developed nearly a century ago in France by Alfred Binet, led to the notion of an intelligence quotient or IQ. The idea had appeal for the American military and for the British eugenics movement and before the middle of this century, a test had been developed to measure virtually every human ability deemed important by North American society. These so-called "objective" tests, placed in the hands of politicians and social engineers of the century, have helped to "prove" time and again such popular beliefs as the intellectual inferiority of women, blacks, and the lower classes. Many educators and researchers argue that things are still the same today.

In a society that feared racial, class, and gender differences, standardized testing became the best tool to reinforce a belief in "standard" or "uniform" skills or behaviors. When Sputnik was launched in the sixties, the testing machine in America accelerated its pace to compete with the Russians. Today, it's the Japanese we're watching. Regardless of the threat—Communism, the ability to compete in a global economy, the dwindling gross national product—standardized tests have been called into the schools to report on our educational well-being. The most widely used tests of recent years, and the most politically popular, are school achievement tests. Also known as "benchmarks" or "outcomes" tests, they are used to measure how well Jane or Raul performs to grade-level expectations. Although the idea has appeal for policy makers and the public, a growing number of teachers and parents are voicing concern about the misuse of these measures. They claim that tests are simplistic, biased political tools that give us little information and, worse, distort teaching and learning. Further, they argue that testing exploits parents' fears about education and undermines their faith in their children's abilities.

> ...tests are simplistic, biased political tools that give us little information and, worse, distort teaching and learning.

Let's try a few questions ourselves.

Question One
Which best describes education for you?
a. an assembly line
b. a treatment center
c. a training center
d. none of the above

a. The industrial model imagines our children as mechanical bodies on a thirteen-year (or more) conveyor belt. As the children pass from one station to the next, we make sure they all receive equal numbers of the necessary parts, assuming that when their schooling is over, they will, in true GM fashion, be ready for the road. Testing along the way is a form of quality assurance, making sure each child's fan belt or gear shift works the same as the others'. The tests assume, of course, that our children all operate with the same working parts.

b. The medical model sees difference between children as indicators of deficiency and therefore, cause for treatment. Assessing what Allison does not know provides evidence of what ails her educationally, and what treatment is required to cure her. Parents know that marking Allison's height on the wall every year will not make her grow faster. Although we would never think to blame Allison for her physical growth rate, we typically blame her, not the educational context, for what she doesn't know. In fact, the medical model, which holds sway most powerfully for children with special needs, convinces parents and teachers alike that difference is a pathological condition, a disease, an aberration from a so-called "norm." No one will disagree that some children have dramatic physical, emotional, or intellectual challenges in their lives; these children require extra resources to support their learning. What many educators and parents are beginning to say, however, is that the emphasis ought to be on the education of these children, not on the often unnecessary and inappropriate testing, labeling, and paper-gathering that take time away from learning and erode a child's sense of worth.

c. The most popular metaphor for education is the training center, a place where children, like caged animals, learn to press the right buttons to receive their reward. The rewards range from stickers to smiley faces to gold stars to scholarships. Those who don't perform as required receive frowns, F's, the threat of being held back, or continual reminders of their status in the academic basement. Advocates of the training model believe strongly that positive reinforcement gives children something to strive for, and that learning to achieve in this way prepares children to succeed in the competitive world ahead of them. Achievement tests are a part of this process, and are the best known educational tool for promoting competitiveness over cooperation, not only between children but within school districts and provincial departments as well. Test scores allow Petra's parents to compare her achievement with Jollene's and with other children in grade three. Many business leaders today disagree, however, claiming that what Petra needs to succeed in her job and in her community is the ability to work with others. Researchers are calling for less competitiveness in schools for another reason; it seems a cooperative environment results in better quality education for girls and for traditionally marginalized groups. At a time when more and more teachers and parents are pushing for non-competitive sports and learning activities in schools, achievement tests are beginning to look like the last holdover of the Industrial Age.

Question Two
Achievement tests are useful because:
a. they are an objective measure of basic or fundamental skills
b. they put all children on an equal footing
c. the results are quantifiable and easily reported
d. none of the above

a. Certain tests can be useful to measure learning. A written test, for example, is a useful indicator of a driver's knowledge of the rules of the road. But before a driver is issued her license, she is also tested on her application of the rules in real driving situations. The real test continues years afterwards, when the driver is on her own tackling routine or hazardous driving situations.

Knowing the formula for measuring the area of a square is one thing: being able to calculate how much carpet you need in the room and how much it will cost is another. An achievement test can measure whether we know the basic rules of the road or a fundamental mathematical formula, but the danger in interpreting the test score is to assume that knowing a piece of information is knowing how it works.

What is basic or fundamental is also cause for debate. How many of us can remember now what a gerund is? Or an oligarchy? Will we need to know the answers to those questions from memory in ten years, or twenty? As parents begin to question the usefulness of school learning, they are realizing that what was basic for them twenty years ago will not be basic in a society in which information increases by the hundredfold daily. Not only will our children need to read and write and do math but they will need the ability to think critically, understand global issues, and learn to work in a diverse and rapidly changing society. Our basics are not their basics, and yet most achievement tests have failed to keep pace or to ask the important questions: basic to whom? and for what?

> ...yet most achievement tests have failed to keep pace or to ask the important questions: basic to whom? and for what?

b. Standardized achievement tests are seductive in their claim that all children will start from the same footing. In fact, we now know that while David or Ali may be a math whiz, it is Daria who thinks and responds musically, Benjamin who is verbally capable, and Kerrilyn whose artistic abilities shine. As a species we have multiple intelligences—both Euro-American and African-American researchers have known this for a decade—and achievement tests are universally biased toward children with strong verbal and mathematical intelligences. When we accord too much weight to these tests, we diminish the value of the visual, athletic, mechanical, social, musical, and other abilities of our children, the very qualities we value in a well-rounded adult and that are necessary for balance in our own lives. We need look only at where the budget axe falls in education nowadays—music, art, and physical education—to see how short-term bean-counting to cut costs has been ignoring the higher long-term costs to a child's spirit or to the social health of a country. What's more, the testing machine is one of the most expensive line items in the budget of most school boards.

It is true that standardized achievement tests put certain groups of children on the same footing: North American urban middle-class children. Test-makers have been working furiously for two decades to create culturally-sensitive tests, using questions that claim to take into account whether a child is from a small African-Canadian or Mi'kMaq community, a working class district, or any other "non-mainstream" group. And at the other end of the scale, test-makers have jumped on a cultural literacy band-wagon, arguing that knowing certain "facts," such as the origin of the terms "Pandora's box" or "Achilles' heel" is necessary to be considered literate in North American society. Critics of both camps say that these attempts are both futile and biased: reducing our real world knowledge and our heritage to a simple score on a test in a multicultural, multiracial society is the end, not the beginning, of equal opportunity. The test is a reflection of the culture in power, no matter how much we tinker with it. And, since most tests are based on the notion that children are more alike than they are different anyway, devising a variety of culturally-sensitive tests undermines the belief in uniformity that drives testing in the first place.

c. The greatest appeal of the achievement test is its ease of scoring and reporting. In our soundbite society, ten-second soft drink ads and two-minute "in-depth" news reports have increased our appetite for the quick answer. What's learning if it can't be scored? Joey got 47 on the grade 12 math test, and Jade scored 80. Obviously, Jade is better at math, or is she? Two issues are key here: first, can a single score tap anyone's full knowledge of a subject or even their potential for learning it? (Perhaps Jade excels at just the kind of question the test uses, and does not know how to apply the concepts; perhaps Joey wrote the test under emotional stress.) Second, are we willing as parents to accept overly-simplistic criteria to evaluate our children, criteria we would not use to evaluate a mechanic, a politician, a potential partner, or even ourselves? Would any of us have agreed to write a Parent Aptitude Test and have our lifetime careers as parents determined by the outcome? Would we agree, in our own jobs, that the complexity of our work can be reduced to one hundred items on a set of tests?

> ...are we willing as parents to accept overly-simplistic criteria to evaluate our children, criteria we would not use to evaluate a mechanic, a politician, a potential partner, or even ourselves?

But reducing achievement to a score, just as reducing voter preference to a pollster's simple number, appeals to many of us, especially to politicians and bureaucrats. Whether or not the numbers reflect the quality of the schooling or the nature of the learning, the numbers can be used to make a case for the political will of the time. Usually, that will involves continuing to stoke the fires of discontent about schools, and to ensure that the results point not at policy makers but at school districts, teachers, and the rise of the single-parent family.

Question Three
Testing will continue because:
a. it is a cost-effective way to measure learning
b. it is scientific
c. there are no alternatives
d. none of the above

a. The testing industry in North America runs into the billions of dollars every year and is operated mainly by corporate testing services with large research and development alliances. Testing is a business, not an educational enterprise. Howard Gardner, a noted Harvard psychologist, argues that more money is spent in psychological circles testing and ranking children than on helping them. If we took the money we are currently using for testing and used it to reduce class sizes and increase support for teachers, he claims, we would see more improvement in student achievement. Supporters of most tests argue that using the results judiciously will, in the long run, improve schools, but this argument has been used for thirty years. Perhaps it's time to redirect the money to areas that are known to make a difference in student achievement.

b. The public still believes in the outdated notion that test scores are the most scientific way to determine student achievement. But science, as we know, isn't any more objective or value-free than any other enterprise. In fact, some researchers are now claiming that unless we look at

> ...more money is spent in psychological circles testing and ranking children than on helping them.

learning as complex, ongoing, and often situation-specific, we are not being scientific at all. A wise teacher's observation or a parent's intimate knowledge of a child is often a more reliable indicator of learning.

c. It is important to make a distinction between testing and assessment. We need to know how children are progressing. But we have a number of alternatives to find out what they are learning and what needs to change. Anecdotal reporting, detailed accounts of what children are doing in class, is now beginning to replace the antiquated graded report card, although the change is very slow. Many parents still want to see a letter grade; it's something they remember from their own school days. But today's teachers are not only more educated about evaluation, they are also more conscientious about providing parents with complete descriptions of Billy's progress. They know that a letter grade, just like the strap, isn't the simple answer it used to be.

Schools are beginning to look at assessment not as a separate activity from teaching and learning, but as part of the landscape. Just as a carpenter measures informally but regularly, stopping to eyeball the structure in progress, or just as the cook adjusts seasoning while preparing the meal, expert teachers are now keeping written and mental records of what children do each day, adjusting their teaching according to what they see.

> Just as a carpenter measures informally but regularly, stopping to eyeball the structure in progress, or just as the cook adjusts seasoning while preparing the meal, expert teachers are now keeping written and mental records of what children do each day, adjusting their teaching according to what they see.

In many classrooms, the portfolio is replacing the single project or test of a child's growth. Nine-year-old Nolan keeps a folder of all his writing since September, his rough drafts, the teacher's comments, and his classmates' responses. As the portfolio grows, so does the teacher's understanding of all the facets of Nolan's writing. Instead of a single writing test, the teacher has long-term evidence of what Nolan has learned and what skills he must continue to work on.

The same teacher watches Christina and assesses her understanding of math. Christina is building a model pyramid and the teacher observes how she uses her understanding of measurement to build an object. The teacher may give Christina a short quiz to assess her skill in computation, and may ask Christina and other children to solve a mathematical problem by writing about it. All such information can be collected in the portfolio the teacher keeps on Christina and other children. This ongoing assessment, the teacher believes, is not only more thorough, but more accurate than a single score on a standardized test.

Question Four

As a parent, I can:

a. ask whether more than one form of assessment is being used to describe my child's learning in all subject areas

b. ask whether the teacher and the school use the assessment to plan teaching and to change curriculum to meet students' needs

c. watch how my child learns in everyday activities where she applies her knowledge to solve real-world problems

d. ask whether time is spent in school on music, art, social, and physical activities so that all children have a chance to shine

e. ask to include my child in the parent-teacher interview to talk about his progress (just as I might be included in my own performance appraisal at work)

f. ask that my child be exempted from all standardized tests if I am uncomfortable letting the school administer such tests to her. I have that right as a parent and as a taxpayer.

g. ask to see my child's file and arrange a meeting if I am concerned that test results in the file have distorted the school's assessment of his true ability

h. think of assessment like photographs in the family album: they are not the final result. Learning and growth are lifelong activities.

i. remind myself that I know my child better than anyone. Schools and tests see only certain sides of a child. I can inform teachers and administrators of what I believe is important about my child's learning. Most are grateful for the information and want to work with parents.

j. all of the above

PUBLIC EDUCATION
...AND FAST

FILLING IN TIME ON THE AIRPLANE, I turn to a *Globe and Mail* piece on education. Sure enough, another rant from Canada's self-appointed education critic. You know who I mean; the cranky ex-teacher who seems to want to promote himself more than to promote educational reform. Has anyone ever asked this guy, I wonder, why he left teaching instead of staying in it and showing others how it ought to be done? Never mind, I mutter to myself. Would you want your child to be taught by someone with opinions on education that are equivalent in virtuosity and range to the average wall switch?

But what is this? He understands that perhaps invented spelling might be all right in some circumstances, especially for children who are learning sound-symbol correspondence and use this approach as a beginning step toward conventional spelling. Now, he continues in the next paragraph, if only all those whole-language advocates would realize this, instead of outlawing sound-symbol work in their classrooms as they have been these many years.

Hello? I look at the date on the newspaper just in case the attendant mistakenly handed me a copy trapped behind the cockpit for the last decade. Is there a glimmer of understanding here?

Does this mean that this fellow is expanding his repertoire of black and white to perhaps a touch of gray? Or does this mean—and I shake my head at the extent of my own cynicism—that all along he has been pulling the collective leg of educators, demanding and capturing the public's attention for the last several years with his Rumpelstiltskin-like rhetorical tantrums so that now he can position himself as the moderate one, the reasonable one, the savior of public education?

I close the newspaper without bothering to cut out the article. Like so many educators, I am weary of the whole-language debate and tired of answering questions

We need a curriculum for educating the public.

from confused parents and neighbors. I admit I am helpless at defending the zealous, inflexible positions of colleagues who, ironically, do not fare so well when they step out of the academy and into a classroom of their own. And I wince at the terrifying words of Ken Goodman, quoted at a conference at Mount Holyoke a few years ago, and recorded in my journal as the date I ducked out of the Umbrella: "We now know how to teach all children." But mostly, I am weary of the assault of ill-informed media stories about skills versus whole language, drill versus experience-based learning, the trendy versus the traditional.

Whole language is not simple. Basic skills are not simple. Learning how to read and write is as gray a territory as any we can name, and likely always will be. We may have a few answers, and we may be asking better questions, but teaching remains complex, and literacy learning and teaching at the end of the millennium can only become more challenging, not less.

> Learning how to read and write is as gray a territory as any we can name, and likely always will be.

As educators, I believe we are up to the challenge. We are better in our profession at recognizing the cultural, social and political influences in literacy learning and teaching. We are better at accepting complexity, at looking through the prism from as many angles as possible. And I think we are better at working together to find solutions, to reach across disciplines and school districts to share our knowledge. Even more hopeful is our growth in teacher-led inquiry, enabling us as professionals to rely less on imported knowledge, and more on the wisdom of our practice and our observations. We are educating ourselves as we educate our students.

But we are failing in our attempts to educate another critical and influential group. When it comes to our communications skills outside the classroom, we just do not make the grade. We need a curriculum for educating the public.

As I read the umpteenth article on whole language that day on the plane, I realized my despair was not about the attack. I enjoy a good argument, and can handle a debate quite handily when all of the issues are out on the table. Here, however, as with most articles on education I read in newspapers and magazines, the issues are not clarified, they are only simplified for the McNews "soundbite" generation of readers. And I am frequently astonished at the quotes from so-called "experts" in reading, people whose names I have never heard, and whose work I have never read. Where is the media digging up these sources? Am I living in another universe altogether?

What they will report is an outrageous case of violence in a local classroom...any story about curriculum is usually a story of failure, and usually the failure of the "new school of thought."...No medium, whether it is the newspaper or a weekly television program specializing in exposés, has ever seriously examined literacy learning...

A story about the information highway is never more than a page away. Nor is a story about the breakdown in universality in our social programs in Canada. The latest in sports scores and team trading is news—seven in the morning, off-the-top of the headline news. And we can always count on an update on the Quebec situation, Oprah's weight, the latest in a patronage controversy, or a conflict-of-interest scam. These stories are news. What's happening in education is not.

WHAT IS GOING ON HERE AND WHAT CAN WE DO ABOUT IT?
A conversation I had with the editor of our local newspaper
was instructive. No, he demurred; we really do not need a
regular column on education: our reporters can cover the
stories out there. But these are times of flux, of cutbacks, of
restructuring, of strikes, anger, and dissent, I argued. Your
paper needs to cover education not by teacher-bashing, but
by a balanced, in-depth look at some of the issues. How
about an occasional story describing a curricular innovation, I suggested. People do not know what is going on in
classrooms, and that includes your reporters, I continued.
You are publishing stories that are sensational, simplistic,
and hopelessly stuck in the sensibilities of the fifties. My
words were ignored.

Let's face it, folks. Education stories and issues are
not hot enough, not sexy enough, for the media. What they
will report is an outrageous case of violence in a local
classroom; but rarely do we read about the issues surround-
ing violence, the programs attempting to reduce the problem, the analysis that connects such violence to larger social
and political forces of which the public are already aware.
Similarly, any story about curriculum is usually a story of
failure, and usually the failure of the "new school of
thought." No critic or journalist, to my knowledge, has
approached the classroom as a cell in a larger organism, a
living microcosm of what's happening out there only
bigger, deeper, and wider. No medium, whether it is the
newspaper or a weekly television program specializing in
exposés, has ever seriously examined literacy learning, for

example, in the context of the cultural forces that will render traditional "basic skills" hopelessly inadequate and ludicrously irrelevant. And no journalist has faced his or her (but usually his) two most frequent lapses in logic. You know the ones I mean: first, today's adult illiteracy problem is a result of today's literacy teaching (come again?); and second, we need schools for the future that operate on the hierarchical, teacher-centered, skills and benchmark programs of the past (…and again?).

The issue of what's happening to news itself is an issue for another essay. Journalist friends of mine lament the increase in the public's appetite for McNews, and the media's willingness to provide such stories. Other media critics, following Noam Chomsky, warn that transnational organizations that own the newspapers will only publish the news they, in their world view, deem fit to print and, in so doing, "manufacture consent." Still other social analysts believe that corporate powers support ongoing attacks on schools and education in order to divert attention from their responsibility and failure to create employment.

ADD TO THESE POWERFUL FORCES—if, as it seems, they do exist—the tendency of educators to take such criticism without complaint, and it is easy to see why education does not fare so well. As a profession, we are not fighters. We dislike controversy, we find public displays of anger or resistance distasteful, and we generally do not raise a fuss, either inside our staff rooms or out of them. We distrust the media, with good reason, and the remnants of soft core socialism have us see the actions of all journalists and business people as unauthentic, insincere, and opportunistic. Oh, we talk: we complain and natter and wave our arms in the air with our colleagues over lunch. We do The Tempest, but in a teapot, and far away from the main stage. And when all is said and done, it is said and done by someone else.

We do not like to call attention to ourselves. It's a hard fact, but it's true. Most of us are unwilling or fearful about speaking in front of a room full of adults. Few will speak to a gathering of colleagues, and most educators are self-conscious about having another adult see them at work in the classroom. We worry about the phone call from the angry parent, the rumor from the board office, the casual comment by the principal in the hallway. Have we done this to ourselves, or has this rock-bottom professional esteem been manufactured elsewhere?

> We need to tell our success stories, inform the public about issues, and learn to use the media as they have used us.

Likely, it does not matter. What matters is that we recognize the future of education may lie in our ability to call attention to ourselves, to educate the public about what we are doing and what needs to be done. We need to tell our success stories, inform the public about issues, and learn to use the media as they have used us. As the saying goes, if not us, then who? If not now, then when?

Many teachers I know do not hold their noses at the idea of self-promotion or of speaking out. Only last week, we attended our son's class performance of two plays the children had written with their teacher, each play a culmination of work done on a bears theme and a sea animal theme. The sets were magnificent, each part carefully painted and mounted by the children. The performance, held in the morning, drew parents from work and filled the audience. After the production, we were invited to coffee and cookies and a visit to the classroom where all the children's work on these themes—math, science, language arts—were displayed on the walls, on display boards, on the desks, and hanging from the ceiling. The morning was a celebration of their learning, but as a parent, I could tell much about the teacher's pedagogy and the classroom climate from what was displayed and how the children responded. Each parent who attended had a positive comment. "I didn't realize they were studying these animals." "We didn't learn about this when I was this age." "My heavens! You didn't tell me you could write this well!"

This event may be common in schools, but not common enough. Unlike many school displays, this event was intimate enough to invite discussion. Our son's teacher promoted the children and their learning, but in doing so, took a huge step in creating community confidence in her ability as a teacher. This event, combined with her regular monthly newsletter and at-home packages for parents who want to work with their children, has situated Kathy Fletcher in this small community as an educator who cares about her students and wants to do the best for them educationally.

I use her name here, intentionally. Just as I use the names of teachers when I write a positive letter to the editor or when I am writing for publication. True, those who read my work are also educators; but this, at least, is a start. I also write letters, talk to newspaper editors, journalists, and business groups. Whenever possible, I find ways to dismantle people's assumptions and unexamined biases about education today.

But how does a busy classroom teacher educate the public? Many teachers, like Kathy Fletcher, write newsletters home. Others, in communities of new North Americans or non-reading parents, hold coffee meetings at the local doughnut shop or library where the children can attend as well. Teachers who bring in parents as assistants reap the benefits of a community member who now has first-hand knowledge not only of the good work being done in that classroom, but the challenges the teacher faces, and typically, that individual will spread the word. A career day in an all-black school in Nova Scotia enabled children in the school to see black Nova Scotians as successful church ministers, nurses, pilots, an Olympic boxing contender, teachers, and engineers. Even better, the guests were able to learn about the resources at the school.

The possibilities are endless, and they needn't take up much time. Often the children themselves will do the promotion given the appropriate activity. We can do much within our local community to reach out to parents and the public. We can watch for ways in which the school and our classrooms communicate "welcome" or "stay away." We simply have to decide which message we want to send.

But beyond the local community are members of the general public, those who read the newspaper and watch television. How do we reach into that sphere, change the ways in which the media have been, in the words of one graduate student, "manufacturing contempt" for educators and for schools?

> How do we...change the ways in which the media have been, in the words of one graduate student, "manufacturing contempt" for educators and for schools?

We start with letters to the editor, for one thing. Even a commitment by each teacher to write one letter to a newspaper a year would result, in our province, in 11,000 letters, many of which would be published. We become aware of how the media read the world, which is not the way we read ours. The daily ebb and flow of activity results in gains for students over a year and we, as close observers, can see growth as steady and incremental. But the press thinks in terms of events, news flashes, news releases. Knowing this, we can invite a local reporter (even if it is "only" the community newsletter) to cover the Fun Fair, the Science Olympics, the Home and School Association car wash, the visit of the astronaut. We can organize a panel discussion on violence on the playground, and make sure the local cable company or television crew is in attendance. Older students can learn to write press releases, to contact the newspaper regularly about goings-on, and to take photos.

You get the idea. We all do. It is just a matter of convincing ourselves that the effort is worth it. With our professional esteem at an all-time low, with the effects of slashed budgets, and decimated resources, it hardly seems worth our while to be trying new curriculum ideas, let alone writing letters to who knows where. And what can a few letters do when we are faced with the power of governments, for example, to dismantle collective bargaining, remove job security, and enforce curricula we do not agree with?

Understandably, feelings of futility hold us back: it's the "Ya-but" gremlin again. But so, too, does the feeling that our colleagues might believe we have sold out to crass commercial treatments of education, that we are behaving as though we are special, that we are rocking the boat. Holding us back, too, is the smug notion that we, at least, know the value of what we do, and our students know it too, and somehow, somewhere, we will be recognized, honored, given our reward. To defend what we do, to talk about it, is, well, demeaning to a profession as noble as ours.

This, I believe, is the most powerful and insidious argument against educating the public about what we do. It is rooted, I believe, in a pseudo-Protestant ethic, and comes from the same place as "pride rideth before a fall," "don't brag about your grades (or your prize or your scholarship)," "never mind what the others say; you know the truth" and other family favorites our parents served up at the dinner table. And for some reason researchers and social analysts are now only beginning to understand, those messages were served up more frequently to women of our generation.

We must, for our own professional survival, keep trying. Like most writers, I have written a great deal that has not been published. I have told jokes that no one has understood, and made complaints that have not been acted upon. My voice has been lost in a noisy crowd, and my arguments in a meeting ignored. But when it comes right down to it, I do not want others to draw my professional profile, to write my life as a teacher.

And so I, like other educators I know, continue to write, to argue, to speak up, to warn, to brag, to praise, and to announce. My children, I hope, will be taught by my willingness to challenge the injustices I encounter, seek a spotlight for a good cause, and to be alert and aware about the media. I do not want to teach them by my reluctance to step forward. If not me, then who? If not now, then when? And, when you think about it, what else is there to do?

Now, to find a mailing address. I think that critic needs to read this.

ETERNITY'S SUNRISE

SANCTIMONY IS DRIFTING through the halls of literacy education.

"He's a very traditional teacher, you know. Not reflective, or student-centered. His desks aren't even in groups. He needs to change, like us."

In an office downtown, a state board meets with administrators to discuss priorities in testing reform. Everyone agrees that a program of nationwide standardized testing will provide the answers that the public needs.

Elsewhere, a committee of teachers, parents, and administrators faces a hostile group wanting to overturn the decision to adopt a particular reading series. The group is part of a movement responsible for banning *Little Red Riding Hood* because Red brought grandma a bottle of wine in her basket. Censorship, the group believes, is the way to right our educational wrongs.

TEACHING IS AN ENDLESS, SWIRLING DANCE of doubt and determination, details and dreams. Sometimes, when the movement of time and people reaches a feverish pitch and we pause for a moment, we can see the classroom in suspension before us. In that moment, like a dancer poised at the edge of the music, we search for the truth in the movement once again. We try to recall, if only briefly, what brought us to this point in the first place.

For me, William Blake's phrase, living in "eternity's sunrise," captures the essence of the teaching and learning enterprise. We wouldn't teach if we didn't believe in the sunrise, didn't have hope for the human spirit. The children are less well fed, the homes are broken and poorer, crimes borne of difference and indifference abound, and still we teach. The public loses faith in the education system, teaching conditions deteriorate, and the business world makes jokes at our expense, and still we teach. Invested with one of society's greatest responsibilities—to help children learn to read and write and get on in the world —we are accorded the least degree of respect of all the professions. And still we teach.

But outside our classrooms, the larger dance around us is turning and the movement is becoming more frenzied. Political walls are dismantling, brick by well-marketed brick. National boundaries are shifting like sand fortresses in the tide. Technology is giving us exotic friends at a keystroke and information growth is lifting us to new dimensions of understanding. At the edge of the schoolyard, where the wind flattens a fast food bag and a condom[1] against the fence, is the world beyond—in chaos. Life and learning just aren't like they used to be, and for many of us in literacy education, such change is frightening. Sunrise just isn't what it used to be.

TEACHERS WHO UNDERSTAND the larger forces of change in society are the teachers who, in their classroom practice, see beyond the furniture. Such teachers are reinventing their teaching daily, and, while they are gaining confidence in their ability to choreograph their moves in chaos, they continue to be humbled by all that their children and their world teaches them. They stay open to learn. Years ago, Donald Graves warned the profession that our enemy is orthodoxy. Lately it seems, sanctimony and smugness are riding with orthodoxy (perhaps they always did), and the result in our classrooms becomes change for the sake of change. Like the old joke about the day the troops were allowed to change uniforms (Jack changed with Joe, Harry changed with...), moving from a "traditional" teacher to

---

1. This article was the last in a series I wrote for *The Reading Teacher*. The IRA editors insisted I remove the words "condom" and "masturbation" because "teachers would find them offensive." (The irony of censoring an article that discussed censorship was lost on them.) We compromised: "masturbation" stayed (it was key to the issue), "condom" went. I brought the issue of censorship and academic freedom to the IRA Board of Directors and to the Executive Director but nothing was ever done. The cancellation of the column inspired a letter-writing campaign by colleagues, but their protests were in vain.

one with a more fashionable label may just give us a different uniform to wear. It's still a uniform, and it is still issued from an outside authority.

> Ah, say the changed, if you have truly examined your teaching, you are beyond the superficial, such as putting desks in groups and burning worksheets.

> *But, I wonder, have we transcended our appetite for orthodoxy? Do we want change, but only on our terms? If we truly value reflective teaching, should we not value the right to self-determination, for students and for teachers?*

MR. AND MS. GENERAL PUBLIC know that they wouldn't want their social skills or their parenting skills to be judged by a national standardized test. In fact, they might find the idea of such evaluation repugnant, an infringement of their human rights. And yet, the notion of using a test to measure the academic or intellectual worth of their son and daughter (and the nation as a whole) is very appealing. "I want to know where Sally ranks," they claim, even as the world about them shifts. "Give me a label," they say, knowing full well such a label can serve either as a badge or a prophesy in a complex world.

> Ah, say the assessors, we know such tests don't measure everything. But they can measure something, and we can use such tests to modify instruction, and to begin educational reform.

*But, I wonder, do we ever question the ethics of such
judgment—assessment is judgment, after all—and do
we ever question its cost, not only in time and money
away from instruction, but in our collective ability to
remain open to questions that matter?*

IN THE NAME OF FREEDOM AND DEMOCRACY, packs of
reading watchdogs raid schoolrooms and libraries for offensive books. The books, whose themes often bring the
outside world into the classroom, may mention alcohol,
drugs, masturbation, or child abuse. Or, the books may
merely depict families other than the white, suburban
household with an aproned mom and a white-collar dad,
and two blond children. By withholding the books from
their children, these watchdogs hope to clean up America
and return it to its original "apple pie" state. Unfortunately,
as their fear and their dogma increase, so do their demands
for control: rather than work with educators and the public
to provide reading materials that promote freedom and
democracy in the context of responsible teaching, these
watchdogs bark at every perceived sign of danger. Their lust
for control, which extends beyond their own households,
threatens freedom and democracy for all.

Ah, say the censors, we have to remember that books
model values, and we don't want such values promoted in our schools.

*But, I wonder, at what point does democracy suffer,
and how best can we promote critical literacy and social*

awareness? Are we so blind we do not see that on this
continent, and in the world at large, "apple pie" stories
of white, middle-class America are a poor diet for our
children's future?

SUNRISE ISN'T WHAT IT USED TO BE. But every morning, it
still comes, and it looks different to everyone who sees it.
The chaos before us is turbulent and frightening, and when
fear overtakes us, we look for something on which we can
depend. Regardless of how open we claim to be, we still
have a longing for The Answer. We cling to a belief that
furniture arrangement defines the teacher, the conviction
that the right assessment tool connects to the spirit of
learning and teaching, and the naiveté that sanitized book-
lists will stop society from entering the schoolyard.

A belief in eternity's sunrise, as Blake reminds us, is a
willingness to let go of the need to pin things down, to exert
unnecessary control. These are heady, but dangerous times.
Our greatest challenge in literacy education, I believe, is not
theory-building, nor methodology. It's coming to terms
with what we are doing here, with understanding the
delicate balance between the impulse to teach and learn and
the impulse to control others, to bend them to our ways.

Trying to capture the magical "winged life" Blake
refers to, to seal it in a jar, destroys it. We must let go of the
acquisitive impulse, the tendency to tighten our grip on
ideas to the point of extinguishing their life. Searching for
the best test, the One Right Method, the measure of
cultural literacy, or the canon that will survive the century

keeps our eyes inside the classroom, looking downward. Nourishing the spirit of learning for a future of global awareness is not merely a social or cognitive or spiritual enterprise; it is also an ethical and moral one. We are ready now, I think, to look out at the horizon and the days stretching before us and ask larger, deeper questions: How can I help human beings grow and learn in this world, now and for tomorrow? And what kind of person do I provide as an example?[2]

2. I want to thank Dorothy Cebula, Margaret Phinney, Andy Manning, and Lorna Durdle for comments that have contributed to this piece.

REFERENCES

Bateson, M. C. *Composing a Life.* New York: The Atlantic Monthly Press, 1989.

Belenky, M.F.; B. Clinchy; N. Goldberger; and J. Tarule. *Women's Ways of Knowing: The Development of Self, Voice, and Mind.* New York: Basic Books, 1986.

Briggs, J.; and F. D. Peat. *Turbulent Mirror: An Illustrated Guide to Chaos Theory and the Science of Wholeness.* New York: Harper and Row, 1989.

Brookfield, Stephen. "Using Critical Incidents to Explore Learners' Assumptions." In *Fostering Critical Reflection in Adulthood* by Jack Mesirow and Associates. San Francisco: Jossey-Bass, 1990.

Carr, Wilfred; and Steven Kemmis. *Becoming Critical.* London: The Falmer Press, 1986.

Chlebowska, Krystyna. *Literacy for Rural Women in the Third World.* UNESCO: Paris, 1990.

Cochran-Smith, Marilyn; and Susan L. Lytle. "Research on Teaching and Teacher Research: The Issues that Divide." *Educational Research* 19:2 (1990): 2-11.

Crittenden, Danielle. "Let's Junk the Feminist Slogans." *Chatelaine* (August 1990): 38-62.

Egawa, Kathy. E-mail correspondence, 1991.

Eisler, Riane. *The Chalice and the Blade.* San Francisco: Harper and Row, 1987.

Eisner, E. "The Primacy of Experience and the Politics of Method." *Educational Researcher* 17 (5)(1988): 15-20.

Franklin, U. *The Real World of Technology.* (The Massey Lectures). Toronto: CBC Enterprises, 1990.

Freire, P. *Pedagogy of the Oppressed.* Rev. ed. New York: Continuum, 1993.

Gilligan, C.; J. Ward; and J. Taylor. *Mapping the Moral Domain.* Cambridge, MA: Harvard University Press, 1988.

Gilligan, C.; N. Lyons; and T. Hanmer. *Making Connections: The Relational Worlds of Adolescent Girls at Emma Willard School.* Cambridge, MA: Harvard University Press, 1990.

Iacocca, L. "Schools Need to Work on Customer Satisfaction." *Inside Guide* (Toronto: Canadian Airlines International) 4, no. 3 (1990).

Jarrell, Randall. *The Bat-Poet.* New York: Collier Books, 1963.

Johnson, Susan Moore. *Teachers at Work: Achieving Success in our Schools.* New York: Basic Books, 1990.

Lortie, D. C. *Schoolteacher: A Sociological Study.* Chicago: The University of Chicago Press, 1975.

Marriott, Vaughn. *Transition.* Unpublished paper. Mount Saint Vincent University, 1990.

McNeil, L.M. *Contradictions of Control: School Structure and School Knowledge.* New York: Routledge, 1988.

Neilsen, A. *Critical Thinking and Reading: Empowering Learners to Think and Act.* Urbana, IL: NCTE, 1989.

Ruddick, J.; and D. Hopkins. *Research as a Basis for Teaching: Readings from the Work of Lawrence Stenhouse.* London: Heinemann, 1985.

Shor, I. "An Interview with Ira Shor." *Language Arts* 67 (1990, 4): 342-352.

Shor, I.; and Freire, P. *A Pedagogy for Liberation: Dialogues on Transforming Education.* South Hadley, MA: Bergin and Garvey, 1987.

Walker, Alice. *Living by the Word.* New York: Harcourt Brace Jovanovich, 1988.

White, Connie. *Journeys Home: Finding the Roots of Literacy.* Unpublished papers, 1990.

Whyte, K. "Nobody's Fifteen Feet Tall." *Saturday Night* 105 (1) (1990): 23-29.